The Ultimate Interview

Quickly learn life-changing skills for
job interview confidence and mastery

Mark Harris

Copyright © 2020 Mark Harris
All rights reserved.
ISBN: 9798655404663

DEDICATION

This book is dedicated to Joe, Tim and Peter. May it serve you well.

Contents

Introduction	i
1. Understanding the Recruitment Process	1
2. A Quick Guide to CVs and Job Applications	15
3. Types of Interview	29
4. Your Key Message: How to Sell Yourself in a Sentence	39
5. Cleaning up Your Online Reputation	45
6. Preparation	49
7. Presentation and Dressing for An Interview	55
8. Body Language and Speech	59
9. Answer Interview Questions with Confidence Part 1	68
10. Answer Interview Questions with Confidence Part 2	82
11. How to Ask Great Questions in Interviews	93
12. Being Brilliant at Selection Tests and Presentations	99
13. Beat Interview Nerves and Jitters	109
14. Communicating	115
15. Putting it all Together - The Big Day	121
16. Offer or Rejection	127
17. What Next?	133

Introduction

The secret of getting ahead is getting started.

Mark Twain

Why read this book?

You know there's a job out there with your name on it. You'll be happy, work with a great team, learn and grow as a person and be well paid and respected by your employer. But first you need to successfully navigate the interview process. That can be tough. There are lots of other capable people competing, so you need to have the edge over them.

I'm here to guide you through the interview process. This book will give you the skills you need to do as well as you possibly can in a job interview. You will quickly learn what recruiters are looking for and be able to apply this knowledge straight away. What's more, you will have those skills for the rest of your life, and you can use them in different situations such as sales pitches, presentations, applications for finance and just being able to 'make your point' convincingly.

You may be at the beginning of your career with little knowledge of the job market, or you may have years of experience and are looking to gain an advantage over other candidates when competing for your dream job. Either way I guarantee you will benefit quickly without having to burn the midnight oil!

So, as it says on the cover, if you follow the advice in this book, you will quickly learn life-changing skills to allow you to be confident in and to master job interviews.

What do I know?

In the early 1990s I was made redundant from a management job with a national retailer. While I had interviewed and recruited a lot of people, I had not been interviewed for many vacancies prior to this, other than low-paid jobs where the employer was desperate for staff.

With a young family, I needed to get back in to work, and quickly. But now there was a recession. I applied for hundreds of jobs, did dozens of interviews, but consistently failed to be selected.

I needed to get back in to work, I needed to do something about it. So, I made the decision to become an expert in being interviewed. I devoured books at the library, spent hours in book shops and made lengthy notes—back then there was no internet. I developed a plan of attack.

A friend told me about a job she thought I would be ideal for. It was as a graduate management trainee with one of the largest retailers in the country. The only problem was I didn't have a degree. But I did have some experience and I put my plan into action.

To cut a long story short, over four and a half thousand graduates applied and I managed to get one of the ten places available.

Since then, I have been offered every position I have been interviewed for. I have worked in recruitment and advised major corporations such as Nike, Motorola, American Express, Zurich and Avis on their recruitment process. I have run interview skills workshops for hundreds of job candidates at all levels.

I want to share all that knowledge with you in this book so you can give the ultimate interview.

Overview

Over the coming pages you will:

- Fully understand the recruitment process from the employer's point of view.

- Know how to prepare for an interview.
- Identify and develop your selling points into a compelling message.
- Understand the different types of interview and how to approach them.
- Understand what any question being asked is aiming to reveal and be able to answer it with confidence.
- Have genius questions ready to ask the interviewer that will make you look great.
- Be confident about your appearance and body language.
- Learn the right amount of communication with the interviewing company to make you look good and not be a nuisance.
- Know how to deal with nerves and anxiety.
- Learn skills you can use for the rest of your life.

This book's approach

I want you to master these skills quickly. I make no apology for keeping the text clear and concise. Your time is precious, and you don't want to spend days acquiring these skills. It's my hope that you can read this in one or two sittings. That way you can prepare for your interview and use this book as a reference and checklist.

A word on style

Because of the international nature of recruitment, I have not used any currencies as examples. The company Digital Widget and any companies used for exemplification purposes are fictional and if they do exist, it is coincidental.

I use the terms 'resume' and 'CV' interchangeably.

Any errors or omissions are mine.

***

Now, let's dive in and find out what Apple's Steve Jobs believed was his most important task.

1. Understanding the Recruitment Process

Hiring the best is your most important task.

Steve Jobs

This chapter will take you through the recruitment process from the point of view of your interviewer. You will learn about:

- Why it's important they get the right person
- The reasons why they recruit
- Needs analysis
- The job description
- The person specification
- Who is involved and their motivation

The primary goal of recruitment

The primary goal of a recruiter is:

To recruit a person who will quickly start delivering results, who will work happily and harmoniously with colleagues, is keen to learn and develop their role for the benefit of the organisation, is positive and resilient, and will be a great ambassador for the organisation.

Of course, a lot depends on the organisation and what they are willing to invest in their employees, but I defy any person recruiting to say they disagree with the statement. Keep it at the front of your mind.

The rules of engagement

It would be difficult to take part in a sport if you didn't understand the rules of the game you were playing. Top sportspeople understand and study their own game intimately, as well as that of their opponents to determine exactly what they have to do to get the greatest advantage.

There are many different types of employers. Some are highly professional; others are incredibly amateurish.

I will be describing what I consider to be the gold standard recruitment process. It will vary depending on the recruiting organisation and their experience, but you should understand how the best do it.

Take off your shoes

I am going to ask you to try a small exercise. I want you to step out of your shoes and into those of an employer.

Imagine you run a small business. You have been going for a couple of years and you are bringing in a fair income. It becomes apparent to you that if you had some extra help, you could do a whole lot better.

You calculate that if you do employ someone on a fair salary, you could double your own personal income and have more free time. You would need to spend money equipping them, you would not be generating income while you train them, but the pay-off could be great.

However, if the new hire doesn't perform, your personal income will reduce by the salary you are paying them plus the investment in recruiting them. *Ouch*.

So, stepping back into your own shoes, you can see there is risk and cost attached to employing someone. It is vital you get the right person.

This doesn't just apply to businesses. It also applies to non-profit organisations. Employers are desperate to get the right hire for a job.

Let's hold that thought and look at why employers recruit in the first place.

Reasons for recruitment

There are generally three reasons why an organisation recruits:

1. They are growing so they need more people.
2. They are restructuring and need to fill new roles.
3. Someone has left and they need to replace them.

Needs analysis

The first task a good organisation will undertake is an analysis of what they need. In the case of growth or restructuring, this will often flow out of their plans. In the case of replacing someone they will ask:

- Do we need to replace them?
- Could someone in the organisation do all or some of these tasks?
- What could have worked better before?

Let's imagine someone, we'll call them Sam, has left a job in sales support from a fictional company called *'Digital Widget'*. The team decide that some of Sam's former responsibilities can be done by the salespeople and draw up a list of the main outputs required. Sam was also a bit unreliable in terms of timekeeping, and this, on more than one occasion resulted in customer complaints. Sam was also a bit grumpy with the salespeople and never really embraced the new Customer Relationship Management (CRM) software, preferring to use spreadsheets—in fact, Sam was a bit of a pain and Digital Widget is excited about getting a replacement!

Having identified the needs, they will draw up a job specification and a person specification for a new Sales Support Executive.

Note: This may be nothing like the role you are seeking, but the principle applies across all job types.

Job description

The job description describes the role in terms of function, tasks, responsibilities, and relationships along with the required knowledge, skills, and abilities. It will describe the working environment and location.

The job description is used in the recruitment process to develop a person specification and later during appraisals and reviews to see if the employee is performing as required.

The following is an example of what the Sales Support Executive's job description might look like—I have kept it brief to save you time!

Title:	**Sales Support Executive**
Grade/Salary:	35,000 pa
Responsible to:	Sales Support Manager
Key Internal Contacts:	Sales Support Manager
	Sales Support Team
	Sales Personnel
	Service Delivery Team
	Finance Team

Key External Contacts: Prospects and Customers

Main Purpose:

> To assist the sales team ensuring they have the resources and support to achieve their sales targets.

Key Outputs:

1. To liaise with sales personnel ensuring they have the materials and technology to prepare and carry out effective sales presentations;

2. To quickly retrieve sales data from sales personnel and ensure that timely quotations are prepared;

3. To keep the CRM updated and inform the sales pers such updates;

4. To swiftly pass closed sales to finance for invoicing;

5. To be the main point of contact for customers after the sale has been closed and to facilitate a smooth transition to the service delivery team;

6. To prepare and circulate regular information/newsletters, on behalf of the company, to prospects and customers;

7. To produce regular reports and present them at the monthly sales meeting.

Other Duties:

Digital Widget operates flexibly where all staff try to help each other, as such there may be a requirement to support other service areas.

Conditions of Service:

1. The post is subject to a 6-month probationary period and one month's notice by either party, subject to the minimum statutory requirements.
2. The post is based at our head office in Metropolis.
3. The post holder will be required to comply with the company's Health and Safety Policy.

Person specification

The person spec describes the experience, qualifications, skills, and personal attributes the company feels will be needed to carry out the assigned duties. This is the main document that will inform the job advertisement, the shortlisting matrix, and the interview questions.

Here is a brief example:

Job Title: **Sales Support Executive**

Department: **Sales**

E = Essential, D = Desirable

Criteria	Standard	E/D	Measure
Work Experience	At least 1 year working in a sales department	E	CV
	Experience of working with multiple departments	E	CV/Interview
	Experience of producing reports	E	CV/Interview
	Experience of presenting reports	D	CV/Interview
	Customer service	D	CV/Interview
Qualifications	Any business-related course or qualification	D	CV
Skills	MS Excel or Google Sheets	E	CV/Test
	MS PowerPoint or Google Slides	D	CV/Test
	Salesforce or similar CRM	D	CV/Interview
	Ability to communicate clearly in writing and orally	E	CV/Test
Personal Attributes	Positive, cheerful, and keen to learn	E	Interview

The matrix

The matrix is essentially the job specification with an additional column that identifies if the applicant meets the criteria or not, or if they do to what degree. There may be additional rows, for example I always put a 'gut reaction' row and a 'team fit' row.

When selecting candidates at the application and interview stage, it's a simple case of looking at the scores and those that score highest rise to the top—I'll describe this in more detail shortly.

Publicity

Digital Widget needs to market the vacancy to attract candidates and this is done in one or more of the following ways:

1. **Internal advertisement** to existing staff who may be interested or know someone who might be.
2. **Trade press** - an advert in Widget Monthly would attract experienced staff from the competition or allied businesses.
3. **General press** - a local or regional newspaper would attract staff in the proximity of the business.
4. **Online** - through job websites.
5. **Agency** who will produce a shortlist of candidates they feel match the requirements of the vacancy.

Where the best candidates might be

It is likely the ideal candidate is working in a similar role for a competitor in the same or a similar industry. A person already working in a similar role and industry may be approached by an agency or by the company itself—this is 'headhunting'.

Often, word of mouth plays a large part. For example, an existing employee may have worked with someone in a previous job or a person is well known in the industry. If Digital Widget approach someone from a competitor, this is known as poaching.

The ideal person might be an existing employee working in another department or part of the country.

Think back to when you imagined running your own business: if you employ someone and they work out, the pay-off could be great but if they don't, your personal income will be reduced.

Try this short exercise: you receive a number of applications, which three applicants are you most likely to want to meet?

1. No experience in your business sector, but with some administration experience.
2. Works for a similar business in a similar role and is moving to your area.
3. Works for your competitor across town.
4. Worked in a similar role for a similar company a year ago and has been working as a volunteer for the past 8 months.
5. Works in a similar role, but a different business sector.
6. Worked in a similar role for a similar company a year ago and has been unemployed for the past 12 months.

The chances are you will have definitely chosen 2 and 3 and you might be trying to figure out which of the others you would like to meet.

It might be that 2 and 3 require higher salaries and your competitor would be delighted to get rid of 3. You might be attracted to 4 who has the experience and has been volunteering or 5 who has done a similar role but for a different business type. You might be wondering why 6, who has experience, has been unemployed for a year and concerned that 1 may not be up to speed quick enough.

There are no correct answers as such, but most recruiters would probably choose 2, 3, and 4 and would be curious about getting 6 in to meet.

The point to understand is this: in the first instance, recruiters, and you if it was your own business, will want reassurance that the people they are considering for a role are 'safe' and the recruitment goal is met.

Matching CVs and application forms

When people respond to the job advert, they will return a CV and cover letter or an application form or a combination of the three.

The recruiter will then use the decision matrix or person specification to filter down the list of applications.

E = Essential, D = Desirable

Criteria	Standard	E/D	Measure	Y/N Poss
Work Experience	At least 1 year working in a sales department	E	CV	
	Experience of working with multiple departments	E	CV Interview	
	Experience of producing reports	E	CV Interview	
	Experience of presenting reports	D	CV Interview	
	Customer service	D	CV Interview	
Qualifications	Any business-related course or qualification	D	CV	
Skills	MS Excel or Google Sheets	E	CV/Test	
	MS PowerPoint or Google Slides	D	CV/Test	
	Salesforce or similar CRM	D	CV Interview	
	Ability to communicate clearly in writing and orally	E	CV/Test	
Personal Attributes	Positive, cheerful, and keen to learn	E	Interview	

9

The application may satisfy all the essential criteria, but the cover letter may demonstrate a candidate's ability to communicate clearly in writing. The recruiter may well reject the applicant or call them in for an interview to test those skills.

If at this stage, there are plenty of applicants who satisfy both the essential and desirable requirements, it is unlikely that those without desirable attributes will be called for an interview.

On the other hand, if there are only a few applicants, the interview roster will be made up of only those satisfying the essential criteria with some desirable traits.

Questions formally created

As the interview dates approach, questions will formally be drawn up. A good recruitment process will ensure all candidates are asked the same questions so fair comparisons can be made.

The questions will be designed to find out if the candidate has the required skills and could achieve the outputs of the job description. For example, to establish if you would be good at liaising with the sales team an interview question might be formulated as follows: *'Can you give me an example of where you have had to work with different teams in an organisation?'* or to identify if you will update the new CRM (unlike Sam!): *'Tell us about computer systems you have worked with in the past.'*

Questions that address the person specification will be drawn up in the following format: *'It's essential that the sales support executive is positive, cheerful, and keen to learn—even when the going is tough. Would you tell us about a time where you have remained positive and cheerful during a tough time, and also why you are keen to learn?'*

Don't worry about the answers to these questions now.

Questions relating to the individual will be drafted to fill any gaps or identify if there are any weaknesses: *'Your CV doesn't mention report writing and presentations, is this something you have any experience of?'* Again, don't worry about these now, we'll tackle them all later.

It's worth adding that a 'hidden' or unspoken, though very important, element exists and that is 'will you fit in?' Some organisations have a very strong culture and a 'type' of person.

A client company of mine had a reputation for playing hard and partying hard (they put an unlimited tab behind a local bar for their staff at Christmas!). They were also a brash young company so as a recruiter if I sent them a shy middle-aged person who liked early nights, I knew the feedback would be *'Sorry, he's not the right fit.'*

In a similar and very rare vein, another client looking for a graphic designer drew my attention to the fact that they were all strong in their religious faith and any candidates had to be comfortable with saying prayers in the morning with the rest of the team. This potentially ruled out any non-believers or those of a different faith—from the employer's point of view.

Of course, it seems unfair that if a person is perfectly capable of doing a job they are ruled out because of their faith, age or lifestyle preferences.

Indeed, in many countries discriminating on these grounds is against the law, but corporate culture is important and the ability to work harmoniously is valued. Very often the evaluation of whether a candidate would 'fit' is not drawn from explicit questions, but rather a gut reaction and soft questions such as: *'Every summer the company goes away for a weekend of outdoor activities, team-building and a party to celebrate our sales, it can be fairly lively—how do you feel about taking part?'*

Agencies

Companies use agencies to reduce the amount of work in the recruitment process. There are broadly two roles an agency might fill:

Temporary workers - here the agency will be told a client company needs a worker for data entry or stacking shelves or coding JavaScript and the agency will send someone along who they know can do that reliably. The worker will be employed by the agency who will then invoice the client company for the wages plus some profit. At any time, the client company can stop using the worker whenever they want, so their commitment is very low.

Permanent workers - this service provides the client with a list of candidates to interview. In simple terms, the agency does the publicising and searching for candidates along with the matching of applications to the 'matrix' and a screening interview (more of which later). The agency is paid a fee by the hiring company based on a percentage of the first year's salary, which could be between 10 and 20%.

The key points to understand about agencies are:

- Agencies do not find jobs for people; they find people for jobs.
- When they place a candidate (and there can be competition from other agencies) they are well rewarded.
- If they think they can place you, they will be all over you like a rash!
- It's worth having a good relationship with agencies.

The players

You will be interviewed by some or a combination of the following people:

1. **Recruitment consultant or head-hunter** - If you apply via an agency, or are approached by one, you will deal with a recruitment consultant. As we have just highlighted in the previous section, they are motivated (financially) by achieving the recruitment goal.

2. **HR or personnel** - In larger organisations, there will be dedicated human resources (HR) or personnel staff. Their job in the recruitment process is to ensure the process conforms to internal policy and is legal. In general, they will be more skilled at interviewing and running selection tests. When they achieve the recruitment goal, they are seen as professional and reinforce the value of having dedicated HR and personnel staff.

3. **Line manager** - This is the person you will be reporting to and, arguably, the most important interviewer. Their success depends on your ability to do the job well.

4. **Senior management and/or owners** - In smaller organisations, the owners, if they are not your line manager, will often want to meet the people working for their company. Senior management in larger organisations like to have an input. They are both motivated by having good people as it is their money or budget you will be paid from and they want you to make the organisation look good.

5. **The team** - It is not unusual to let the candidate take time with each team member they will be working with. The team want to know they will be working with someone they can get on with day in and day out.

Conclusion

A fair bit to take in, but important because you now have an understanding of the process from the other side of the interview table and this forms the foundation upon which you will build your approach to the interview process.

By thinking about the process from the employer's point of view and looking at a fictional company, you have learnt:

- That it is vital to an organisation's success to recruit the right people
- The reasons why they recruit
- Needs analysis
- The job description
- The person specification
- The matching process
- How questions are drawn up
- Who is involved in the process and their motivation

***

But how do we get to the point where we are asked along to an interview? We'll look at that next.

2. A Quick Guide to CVs and Job Applications

A pessimist sees the difficulty in every opportunity; an optimist sees the opportunity in every difficulty.

Traditional

While the focus of this book is on mastering the interview process, it's only right that we touch on CVs and job applications. This is because your CV will feature prominently in the interview and there needs to be a clear correlation between the first impression—your CV and application letter—and the interview. In this chapter you will learn:

- How to identify if it's worth applying for a job
- The first approach
- How to balance your CV between providing too much information that will rule you out and just enough so the recruiter would like to find out more and call you for an interview
- Application forms
- How to write a good cover letter

Should I apply?

Let's say you see a job advertisement like this, and you like the look of it:

Sales Support Executive

35,000 pa + Benefits

Digital Widget is one of the most exciting companies in the rapidly changing widget sector.

We are seeking a positive and cheerful Sales Support Executive to help our sales team achieve the challenging goals we have set for the next five years.

You will have at least a year's experience working in a sales department liaising with multiple departments and providing great customer service and you will be familiar with producing reports generated from a spreadsheet.

The ideal candidate will have good presentation skills, a business-related qualification, and experience of a cloud-based CRM.

Please apply by email before the 31st of January to hr@widgeco.com.

Your first task is to analyse what they are saying:

In the first paragraph, they say they are an 'exciting company'. This is designed to attract potential candidates—it may or may not be true, but it gives you an idea of how they see themselves. They mention the sector is 'rapidly changing'—this suggests they are facing challenges and employees need to be adaptable.

The second paragraph calls for a 'positive and cheerful' candidate—well, who wouldn't? But the fact they have chosen these words over something like 'hardworking and conscientious' means they are qualities they value, either because the last person did *not* possess them in great quantities (which we know to be the case with Sam) or because the previous holder of the post had those qualities and they were particularly appreciated.

They mention the challenging goals they have set the sales team—an indication that this is probably a pressurised environment—more reasons to be cheerful and positive.

The third paragraph doesn't require much analysis, it is a list of essential skills. The final paragraph is a list of desirable skills.

Draw up a list from the advert, in effect creating your own decision matrix:

- Exciting and rapidly changing
- Positive and cheerful
- Keen to learn
- 1 year in a sales department
- Multiple departments
- Customer service
- Reports
- Spreadsheets
- Presentation skills
- Business qualification
- Cloud-based CRM

For each of these points ask yourself: *'Can I show that I have direct or transferable skills and/or experience for each of these?'*

By transferable skills, I mean skills that were acquired in a different setting. For example, you may have worked in a sales department (direct experience) but not created reports while you were there. However, if you helped out in a voluntary capacity, for example as treasurer or membership secretary at a local club or college society, you might have used spreadsheets to record data and present information at monthly or quarterly meetings. This experience could be applied in a work setting.

Think as widely as possible. You may not have an MBA or a degree in marketing, but, for example, a Google AdWords and/or Analytics Certification is a valuable business qualification in today's digitally-focused business world. They can be achieved in under two days.

You can acquire knowledge and skills using the internet very quickly. Let's say you have no experience of a cloud-based CRM, in fact, you don't even know what CRM means! No problem: google something like 'best CRM software' and have a look at the websites of CRM providers. Look at the demo video and ask yourself if you could get your head around a CRM system—if the answer is probably, then you can tick that box and describe yourself as 'familiar' with it.

If you answer yes to over half the questions, it's worth taking the first steps: calling the company or agency.

The first approach

You don't want to waste your time filling in application forms, crafting cover letters or emails, and tweaking CVs if there is something fundamental missing from your application. Unless the job advert specifically rules it out, you're going to call the company or agency to fill in any blanks and make a positive first impression.

We'll assume you have 8 months experience in a sales department, no formal business presentation experience and you've never used a CRM before.

Draw up a list of questions you want answered, not too many, three or four should suffice:

- Is less than a year's experience OK?
- Which CRM do they use?
- How important is having presentation experience?

Now make a list of impressions you want your interviewer to be left with:

- Positive and cheerful
- Keen to learn

There's no guarantee you will speak with someone who will be making decisions, but this is good practice.

I was once given a tip about public speaking: Before you go on stage, as the audience is applauding, speak out loud to yourself nice and clearly. By doing this your first words on stage will not be a dry croak.

I recommend the same before you make a first call to a company. Say out loud *'Hello, may I speak to whoever is dealing with the Sales Support Executive vacancy?'*

Continue by role-playing the call: *'Hello, my name is [Your name] and I'm keen to learn a bit more about the vacancy you are advertising before I put in an application.'*

Notice what you have done there? You have said *'I'm keen to learn'*. Already, at this early stage, you are starting to plant the right impression and play their words back to them—all in a cheerful manner!

Practise asking your questions and at the end of the call say, *'That sounds really positive, I'll email an application before the 31st.'* Again, you have used the word 'positive'.

Now make the call—don't be a slave to a script and be natural.

When you ask your questions make sure you qualify them: *'I have 8 months experience in a sales department, is it essential applicants have 12 months?'* or *'I have experience of presenting at college meetings, but not in a business setting—do you think that should suffice at this stage?'*

Make a note of the answers and read back for confirmation: *'8 months should be fine'* and *'You'll be asking applicants to do a short presentation, which will identify if I have basic presentation skills.'*

CV/Resume

Your next task is to create a resume, curriculum vitae, or CV. If you have one you can tweak it. If you do not have one, it's good to have a base one to work from.

ALERT: I am often asked if it should be adapted for each job application. The answer is yes. The exception is where you submit one to an agency or organisation speculatively where there is no particular job vacancy. Even then you will adapt it for the type of position you would like them to consider you for.

CV vs. resume

A CV is more commonly used in Europe, the Middle East, Asia and Africa. In the US, a resume is more common. They are, to all intents and purposes, the same thing: A summary of your work experience, qualifications, skills, and accomplishments. You might include interests if there is room and names of personal and professional referees.

Writing rules

1. Use a standard paper size—A4 in the UK and Europe, letter in the US.

2. Most applications will be digital, but If you print it, do so on plain white paper; never be tempted to stand out by using fancy paper—it doesn't scan well.

3. Use a simple readable font: Times New Roman, Arial, Helvetica, Cambria, Garamond are all safe. Never be tempted to use a fancy font to stand out—you will, but for the wrong reason.

4. Try to keep it to 2 pages maximum.

5. Check your spelling, several times.

6. Make sure there are NO negative statements.

7. Generally, third person but can lapse in to the occasional first person—the idea is to sound neutral and objective.

Format

Instead of describing at length the required format for a CV, here is a generic example. I will then discuss each element that is not self-explanatory.

First Name Surname CV/Resume
21 Road, Town, Region. Postcode.
M: 07000 000000 E: you@emailaddress

Personal Statement

A positive and cheerful customer service manager with experience in the manufacturing sector who can work as part of a team and unsupervised. I have experience of working in a business to business environment and with the public.

Work Experience

Oct 2016 to Present – *ZipperCo* – Customer Services Supervisor

> Full-time role working with a major fastening company leading a team of four in the customer services department.
>
> Creating team rota and managing staff performance within allocated budget.
>
> Second-line support for customers on phone and email. Managing customer service database.
>
> Liaising closely with the sales department to provide immediate after-sales support.

Jan 2016 to Oct 2016 – *Promarketing* – Marketing Assistant

> Temporary contract working with a marketing company. Preparing direct mail and coordinating deliveries. Data entry on to customer database.
>
> Employee of the Month April 2016

Jan 2015 to Dec 2015 – *Travelling*

Travelling in Europe and the Middle East - working as a volunteer at various children's charities.

Sept 2013 to Jan 2015 – *Nom Nom* – Waiter

Full-time employee at leading restaurant. Providing excellent customer service, cash handling, providing feedback to management team regarding operational issues.

Skills

- Full driving licence
- Managing Performance Course
- MS Office: Word, Excel, PowerPoint and Outlook
- Customer Soft Administrator

Education & Qualifications

Sept 2011 to July 2013 – *The College*

- Diploma in Business - Merit
- Diploma in Art - Distinction

Sept 2007 to July 2011 – *The School*

- Certificate in Mathematics - Merit
- Certificate in English - Distinction
- Certificate in History - Merit
- Certificate in Science - Merit
- Certificate in Art - Merit

Interests

I like running and am treasurer at my local running club. I am a brown belt in karate. I enjoy reading and drawing.

Recruiters see thousands of CVs and having a clear and relevant document that quickly answers the question 'has this person got the skills and experience?' will be gratefully received. Furthermore, many recruiters scan and import CVs into software, so a clear document will ensure a good scan and require little manual intervention.

CV sections

Think about the job in the previous chapter.

At the head of the page are your name and contact details, nice and clear so you can be contacted quickly and easily.

Your 'personal statement' is your key message (we'll discuss this further in Chapter 4). This is the impression you want to leave so that if someone who read it was asked about you, in an ideal world, they would say: *'Positive and cheerful with management experience in customer services and manufacturing experience—probably worth interviewing.'* Keep this tight and relevant. You will notice from the example that it avoids the first person in the first sentence and uses it in the second. This is to appear objective and neutral without sounding impersonal or cold.

Digital Widget perspective: *This is a positive and upbeat statement, in fact, they've used the same words 'positive and cheerful' as our advert—what a coincidence. It is fairly well aligned to what the vacancy requires—no obvious sales department experience though.*

I personally like a CV to tell me what work experience a candidate has had as soon as possible. That is often the most relevant information to the recruitment process. Remember what we said about the ideal candidate already working somewhere similar. The emphasis on certain elements of your work experience can be tweaked according to the vacancy you are applying for. The second job in the CV above is based on one I had years ago. My job was to drive a scooter to various locations and deliver leaflets as well as targeted letters to certain companies. I used to help plan the route and bundle the leaflets up and enter the locations I had delivered to on the computer—I was a basically a delivery guy. But if you use the language of business, it sounds a bit better! *Preparing direct mail and coordinating deliveries. Data entry on to customer database.*

Digital Widget perspective: *Aha! Although the current job is not in a sales department, it does involve working with the sales department in a similar role to that which is required.*

Where you have a significant gap in your CV, make sure you fill it with something positive. In the example above the applicant travelled for eleven months and worked with children's charities—did the applicant actually travel for all that time, or was it several weekend trips? Was the work with the charities for the entire duration or three charities for a week each? The point is, it is a positive statement and it would be worth finding out more.

Next I want to know what skills you have that might be relevant to the job that could be useful now or in the future. This will include acquired skills and any formal training courses; you could have a separate section for courses attended if you have several that are relevant. And the key is relevance. If you served in the military a 'sniper course' is not relevant to a marketing role, but an 'effective communication' course could be.

Digital Widget perspective: *The software skills requirements are satisfied, there is a business-related course and, on the face of it, a course on a CRM has been taken.*

Your education can come next and more or less emphasis can be placed on it depending, first, on how long ago it was and, second, the level and relevance.

Interests give a potential interviewer more information about you to provide some depth, but crucially assure them you are not a couch potato who collects empty wine bottles and chocolate wrappers.

Digital Widget perspective: *Although the essential requirement to have worked for a year in a sales department doesn't show here, there is enough to suggest at this stage that the applicant would be worth interviewing.*

How much information?

The information you provide should be just enough for the person reading it to say *'OK, they have experience and skills, I want to know more.'*

Do not be tempted to tell them everything that ever happened to as they could rule you out for an interview believing they kn everything they need to know.

If you have limited experience, make sure you draw out transferable skills from interests and education and make the most of the work you have had.

Maybe you have years of experience? If it's not relevant to the application only go back a few years and/or reduce the amount of information as you go back. Confine your education to the most relevant and highest qualifications.

The information you provide must be relevant, at best to the job you are applying for and, at least, to the type of workplace you are aiming at. There is always a danger that too much information can muddy the waters. For example, if you once had an exciting job, it might be active military service, working with a major celebrity or excelling in a sport, this may overshadow the vacancy. While some people may want to interview you out of curiosity, you can avoid being ruled out because they think you'd 'get bored' or would be 'overqualified' by toning down that experience.

So, instead of saying *'Soldier—parachuting behind enemy lines and neutralising enemy combatants'* you might say *'Soldier—supporting colleagues in live operations in combat zones.'* Or rather than saying *'Assistant PA—Helping Kanye West's PA to manage celebrity parties after awards ceremonies, meet and greet'* you could say *'Assistant PA—Event management for VIPs, meet and greet.'*

Don't get me wrong, there is every reason to be proud of your achievements and experience but remember, employers want someone who will passionately embrace the role on offer and there's a risk that if you appear to have peaked you may be passed over. Make someone reading the CV want to know more.

Crucially, you need to be prepared to be questioned on every aspect of your CV. For that reason, it is important to be truthful and while you can adjust the volume on certain facts on your CV, you'll be in dangerous waters if you cannot support your claims in depth—don't be tempted to adjust the volume so much that it appears you are hiding something.

Adjusting the volume: Some years ago, before I did a degree, I would apply for jobs that required the applicant to be a graduate or graduate level. I did have a management qualification that was typically taken by graduates so had no qualms describing myself as a 'graduate-level manager'. I successfully won a place on a graduate scheme without a degree.

Application forms

Some employers require you to fill in an application form. If you already have a CV this can form the base for the information you provide.

Application forms, be they digital or on paper, can request all sorts of information from standard CV content to questions about why you want to work for the company. The scope of this book does not extend to exploring all the options relating to application forms, but a number of general rules apply:

1. Be truthful and relevant
2. Be tidy and clear: ideally type responses if your handwriting is anything like mine—illegible!
3. Use the space provided as a guide to how much information to provide—but don't fill it for the sake of filling it.
4. Make sure you keep a copy of the filled-in form for your own reference.

Cover letter/email

The cover letter gives you the opportunity to match your skills and experience to the needs of the job vacancy. It's here you can add anything not explicit in your CV and sell yourself a bit harder.

If we were applying for the Digital Widget job in the previous chapter and sending the CV above, a cover letter might look something like this:

Dear Sir/Madam,

I am writing to apply for the vacancy of Sales Support Executive advertised in Widget Weekly and enclose my CV.

I am positive and cheerful and have over two years' experience supporting sales staff, reporting to multiple departments, and ensuring customers are delighted with the after-sales service they receive.

I have good skills in all MS Office products and am a certified administrator for Customer Soft.

As an enthusiastic and keen learner, I am confident I would quickly become an asset to Digital Widget.

I am moving to Metropolis next month and can be available at short notice for an interview.

I look forward to hearing from you soon.

Kind regards,

[*Your name*]

The key takeaway from this letter is that it draws attention to attitude, skills, and experience. It makes the confident statement that the applicant is low-risk as they would 'quickly become an asset'. The letter explains why the applicant is looking for another job (moving) and makes two assumptions without being pushy: first that there may well be an interview and second, that they will hear from the company soon—it's amazing how bad some companies are at acknowledging applications.

Conclusion

By reflecting on how to construct a CV and an application letter, you understand there is a clear link between the first impression—your CV and application letter—and the interview. In this chapter you have learnt:

- How to identify if it's worth applying for a job
- The first approach
- How to balance your CV between providing too much information that will rule you out and just enough so the recruiter would like to find out more and call you for an interview
- Application forms
- How to write a good cover letter

***

There are all sorts of interviews you could attend, but what are they and why so many? We'll tackle that next.

3 Types of Interview

*No law or ordinance is mightier
than understanding.*

Plato

Now that we have examined the background to arriving at the interview stage, we'll take a look at the different types of interview you may encounter, their main purpose, and how they are typically conducted.

In this chapter you will learn about:

- The purpose of interviews
- Agency interviews
- Telephone interviews
- Face-to-face interviews
- Video interviews
- Panel interviews
- Second interviews
- Psychometric tests
- Selection days
- In-tray exercises

Interviews—a business meeting

As a starting point, you should be aware that an interview is a business meeting between two parties: one party, the employer, looking for a person to help move them to where they want to be and the other party, you the applicant, having the skills and experience that might help achieve that.

The purpose of the interview is to establish if:

1. You have the right skills and experience
2. The employer is the sort of organisation you would like to work for
3. The terms (pay, conditions, hours etc.) are agreeable to both parties.

Think about selling a product or service. A buyer is looking for a product to make their factory run smoother, the seller has a machine that does that. They meet to discuss what the factory does, what the machine does, and come to an agreement on whether the machine will make the factory run smoother. They will agree on the price, delivery, and maintenance. They will meet several times to discuss details or meet additional stakeholders and at any point the sale process might falter, either because the buyer decides on alternative action or the seller is not happy with the terms.

A job interview is also like going on a date. Both parties meet, talk, discuss interests, discover a bit about each other and see if, after spending some time together, they are attracted to each other enough to continue the process with a second and third date until the point at which they feel comfortable with each other and become a couple… or not. Again, at any point, one or both parties could decide they are not attracted to each other or find out something they are uncomfortable with and stop the process of recruiting a partner. Incidentally, that's where the analogy ends!

The balance of power—arrogance vs. desperation

In a fair world, all job interviews would be a meeting of equals to discuss if they can work together. You should assume this is the case for the following reasons:

1. Where you have the desired skills and experience and the

employer is keen to employ you, the balance of power is tipped towards you. If you are too aware of that, there is a risk that you become arrogant and demand too much. There's a saying in management: *'I'd rather have a hole in my organisation than an asshole.'* So be professional and respectful.

2. Alternatively, you could be interviewed for a job you would love to have, and the employer has numerous candidates who would also love the job. The danger here is appearing desperate and being sycophantic: Be professional and retain your dignity.

Ideally, you will be confident in your skills and experience and, in either scenario, if you would like the job, make it clear to the interviewer as they do not want to employ someone who can take it or leave it.

Typical interview flow

Some jobs are won after one face-to-face interview, but often there are more. It could go something like this:

1. Agency interview
2. Telephone interview with company
3. First face-to-face interview with psychometric test and in-tray exercise
4. Second interview with panel

So, you could encounter more than one type of interview. We'll now describe the format and purpose of each.

Agency interviews

As we have already mentioned, recruitment agencies find people for jobs, not jobs for people. This is important to understand because it never pays to be over-demanding of agencies.

There are a couple of types of interviews you will have with agencies: First, a general interview if there is no particular vacancy on offer. This is to establish if you have the sort of skills and experience for the sort of vacancies that the agency works with. Second, a vacancy-specific interview. An agency is used by an organisation to make the recruitment process easier for the employer and it will present a shortlist of candidates to their client with notes. Something like this:

- Candidate 1 is the most qualified and experienced but is not available for three months and is looking for a 10% greater salary.
- Candidate 2 has worked in customer services working closely with after-sales. Very friendly and positive.
- Candidate 3 is not obviously a contender but works for Widget Corporation in operations and wants a more outward-facing role. Comes across well and is very professional.

These conclusions will be the result of a fairly informal interview where the agency consultant is establishing if they are happy to present you to a client, but also seeking to understand what you want. The consultant wants their client to say *'Thanks, a really good roster of candidates.'* They do not want the client to say *'Why did you send me a candidate who can only work 4 days a week?'* Recruitment consultants need to know all the facts, so they help put you forward and negotiate terms if offers are made.

When I worked as a recruitment consultant, I quickly learnt to ask: *'What is your ideal salary?'* and *'What will you not get out of bed for?'* The reason for this is early on a candidate told me he wanted 25,000 and I didn't put him forward for a vacancy paying 22,000. Not having any candidates from me, the client went to another agency and the same candidate applied for and got the job—my company missed out on a 4,400 commission. Of course, the candidate may not have seen the advert and missed out altogether, so let agencies know your desired salary and minimum and try not to be too bullish, if at all.

Telephone interviews

When recruiting, I almost always do a first interview on the telephone. It allows me to do two things: First, to see how a candidate comes across on the phone and second, to avoid making judgments based on the candidate's appearance. We'll talk more about the 'halo effect' later.

It's important with a telephone interview that you can do the call undisturbed and, if you are using a mobile, that you have good reception. Try a test call to make sure this is the case.

It's worth thinking about the clarity of your voice and the speed at which you speak. The interviewer cannot pick up any visual cues, so you need to be clear and not rushed or monotonous. Try recording yourself to see how you come across.

Face-to-face interviews

This is the most common interview format and the one that we worry about most. Interestingly, a lot of interviewers get nervous about interviewing people, particularly if it is not their main job or don't do it very often.

This is the classic business meeting or business 'date' and often includes HR or personnel staff and a manager who will be working with the individual.

They can vary from the quite informal—in the reception of a hotel—to very formal in an office either side of a desk.

Their main purpose is for you, the applicant, and them, the employer, to meet and see if you have the right skills and experience, if they are the sort of organisation you would like to work for and if the terms (pay, conditions, hours etc.) are agreeable to you both.

Most first and second interviews are conducted this way.

Video interviews

Many face-to-face interviews are now done via Skype, Zoom, Google Meet or other video conferencing apps. These are particularly popular where the vacancy is in another territory or country and increasingly so following Covid 19.

The same rules as for telephone interviews apply here. Make sure you are undisturbed, and your internet connection is solid—not always easy but try a test run with a friend or family member.

If you are using Wi-Fi in your home, turn off all other devices connected to the router, tell family or people you share with not to stream or upload large files during the time of the interview and it should mean you get the lion's share of the available internet service.

If you don't have a great connection, let the interviewer know at the beginning of the call and suggest that you'll call back in if it drops. This will show the interviewer you can think ahead and plan.

Position your computer so you are well-framed, make sure the camera is at eye level, so the interviewer is not looking up your nose or at the top of your head.

It's also worth considering your backdrop. Make sure it is neutral, so your interviewer is not asking themselves questions about your environment.

Panel interviews

While many face-to-face interviews involve more than one interviewer, the panel interview will have several. The purpose of a panel interview is two-fold: First, to place the candidate under more stressful and tougher conditions and second, to allow a wider range of people to meet the candidate and inform the decision as to whom to recruit.

They can be quite tough with some members being friendly and others being very rude or aggressive. This is almost always part of an 'act' to see how you respond to difficult people.

A panel interview may well be a second interview.

Second interviews

A second interview occurs where, obviously, an interview has already taken place and the recruiters have a shortlist of candidates who they think could probably do the job but want to dig deeper. It is normally face-to-face.

Ensure you remain consistent with your answers from the first interview and be prepared to dig deeper with any questions you have.

Skills tests

Skills tests are designed to see if you can do the fundamental tasks of the job. If you say you can use the MS Office suite, you may be asked to carry out some tasks. If you say you are a proficient JavaScript developer, you may be asked to write some code, and if the role requires presentation skills, you may be asked to do just that.

It's important that you don't over-exaggerate your abilities. If it is a while since you have performed a particular task, make sure you get back up to date with the skill.

Meet the team

I like to introduce candidates to the team they will be working with. This helps on two levels. First, it involves the team in the selection of the candidate and second, the candidate gets an idea of the sort of people they will be working with. I normally do this when I am down to the last two or three. It will involve around five minutes with the people you will be working with every day and it is an opportunity for you to ask questions about the job and what it's like working for the organisation.

Psychometric & aptitude tests

Whilst not an interview as such, many companies use psychometric profiling. Here's a very simple overview of how they should work based on the training I received through the British Psychological Society: Let's say we are recruiting for a salesperson. The test designer will find a bunch of really successful salespeople. The salespeople will be asked a lot of questions, and the answers will be aggregated. The results then tell us how successful salespeople typically answer certain questions, they are a profile. When a test subject is asked the same questions, the results are compared to the profiled answers and the test gives an indication as to how close to the profile group the applicant is.

Crucially, there are no right or wrong answers; the results should form the basis of questions for the interviewer to ask where there are variations between the profiled answer and that of the test taker.

IQ type tests—numerical and verbal reasoning

You have probably seen these types of tests. You are given a series of numbers, letters, or shapes and you have to say which one comes next.

You might also have a comprehension (verbal reasoning) test, which presents a number of statements and asks you to select an answer—the answer may be that you need more information.

Numerical reasoning works along the same lines with… numbers.

In my experience, the more you practise these types of tests, the better you get at them. You may not become more intelligent, but your intelligence muscle will be exercised!

In-tray exercises

The in-tray exercise aims to see how well you cope under pressure and, more importantly, how you prioritise your work.

You will be given a certain amount of time and a pile of jobs that need doing. You may be interrupted during the exercise with another job or 'emergency'. You will **not** be expected to complete them all in the time allotted.

We'll discuss how to tackle them in Chapter 12.

Role-play

The role-play allows the interviewer to see you in a work situation, albeit slightly artificially, and how you react to or approach a situation.

An old classic for salespeople is for the interviewer to ask the applicant to 'sell me this pen'.

Another might be serving an imaginary customer in a retail setting or having to discuss an awkward situation with an imaginary employee.

Some people find role-plays uncomfortable, for all sorts of reasons: the location, the other person, and being observed to name three.

Most interviewers appreciate that role-play can be awkward, and they are as much as anything a test of confidence and thinking on your feet rather than anything else. Importantly, it is not a test on how well you can act unless it is an audition, in which case it is!

Selection days & assessment centres

Selection days are designed to bring together groups of applicants to complete some or all of the activities discussed above. They may take place over a couple of days.

Conclusion

There are a number of different types of interviews and you should be broadly familiar with why they are taking place and how they are conducted.

In this chapter you have learnt about:

- Interviews being a business meeting
- Agency interviews
- Telephone interviews
- Face-to-face interviews
- Video interviews
- Panel interviews
- Second interviews
- Psychometric tests
- In-tray exercises
- Selection days

***

Advertisers understand it, politicians get it. In the next chapter you'll get it.

4 Your Key Message: How to Sell Yourself in a Sentence

If you have an important point to make, don't try to be subtle or clever. Use a pile driver. Hit the point once. Then come back and hit it again. Then hit it a third time—a tremendous whack.

Winston Churchill

In this chapter, you will understand how to craft the key message that you want to get across at the interview. You will learn:

- Why you need a key message or personal statement
- How to create a key message
- Incorporating features, advantages, and benefits (FAB)
- How to ensure the interviewer(s) remember your key message

Why have a key message?

All successful businesses and political campaigns have a strapline or slogan. Whether you like or dislike the products or agree or disagree with the politics, a simple, memorable and often repeated strapline or slogan helps keep companies and politicians at the front of people's minds.

For you the key message is what you want the interviewer to remember about you. Furthermore, your will repeat the message and return back to it when answering questions. It will be seared into your heart and, by the end of the interview, into the interviewer's mind!

The importance of a key message

How would you like to be remembered after an interview? The tall one, the short one, the one in the blue suit or the positive and cheerful one with experience in customer service?

It is important to stand out for the right reasons, to rise above the crowd.

How to create a key message or personal statement

In Chapter 2, we discussed the application process and we drew out key attributes from the job advertisement. Indeed, when we discussed ringing the company, we made a note of the impression we wanted to leave: Positive and cheerful, and keen to learn.

You'll remember the CV said:

A positive and cheerful customer service manager with experience in the manufacturing sector who can work as part of a team and unsupervised. I have experience of working in a business to business environment and with the public.

Incidentally, you'll notice I use the term key message and personal statement interchangeably. This is because your personal statement should be your key message. It's what goes at the top of your CV, it's what you say when asked *'Tell us about yourself'*.

So how do you create it? First, you will look at the job advert or person specification. If you were not provided with this, call the company for one—this is a good move, it shows you are doing research, preparing, and are organised. If they don't have one, work with the job advert and anything else available. See Chapter 2.

As with the job application, we are quite simply going to reflect back key parts of the person specification as we have done in the statement above. You might want to tweak it if you have more information.

Read it out loud, does it sound natural? The statement above bit clunky when read out as we have said experience twice and manufacturing is, by definition, business to business, so you might tweak it accordingly:

A positive and cheerful customer service manager with experience in the manufacturing sector and serving the public. I can work well as part of a team and unsupervised.

Remember when you draw up your key message that employers are looking for staff who:

'Will quickly start delivering results, will work happily and harmoniously with colleagues, is keen to learn and develop their role for the benefit of the organisation, is positive and resilient and will be a great ambassador for the organisation.'

Testing your key message—FAB

FAB stands for Features, Advantage, Benefit. If you work in sales, you will probably have heard of this approach to describing products.

A feature is something the product has. For example, a rubber handle on a knife. The benefit is the knife won't slip in your hand and the advantage is you won't cut yourself; it is safer. A feature of this book is it is fairly short, the advantage is it doesn't take long to read, the benefits are you can put it to use quickly, save time, and get the job you want.

If you have difficulty drawing out benefits, one of the best ways is to ask, 'so what?' A benefit, by definition, means someone gains something; they benefit. I am cheerful (feature). So what? This means people generally like me (advantage). So what? Customers feel relaxed and happy to talk to me (advantage). So what? There are fewer refunds and they spend more (benefit). Very often a benefit will boil down to making money or saving money and time.

A word of warning. Do not say something that is untrue, or you cannot support! To test this, your next task is to justify and support your statement. This may well happen at the interview. Let's take the examples below:

- Would other people say you are positive and cheerful?
- Give an example of how being positive and cheerful has helped your job.
- Describe your customer service manager role.
- Discuss your manufacturing sector experience.

To further test the message, say it to friends and family, ask them what they think.

It's important that you sound natural, not robot-like or as though you are reading from a script. Keep repeating and justifying it out loud—ideally when you are alone!

Getting the message home

We're going to use a technique used by many news broadcasts and documentary and reality shows: We tell them what we are going to tell them, we tell them, and we tell them what we told them. What?

I'll explain. News broadcasts start with dramatic music and the newsreader telling you the headlines: *Four people die in plane crash, Government changes mind on budget, new record set by sprinter at national finals.* Then they tell you the news and at the end they recap.

Imagine a TV show about an adventurer. The voiceover goes something like this: *Jan, who has always lived in the city and hates creepy crawlies, is going to the jungle where there are giant insects, snakes, and wild animals.* You are told what you are going to watch—if there are commercials, this will often be repeated every time the show restarts. (It really annoys me!) Then you watch the show and see Jan from the city in the jungle trying to cope with all the challenges. At the end of the show we are told: *Well, Jan may be a city slicker with a fear of creepy crawlies, but that was no barrier...* and so on!

Let's role-play this approach in an interview situation:

Interviewer: So, tell me a little bit about yourself.

You: I'm a positive and cheerful customer service manager. I have experience in the manufacturing sector and serving the public. I can work well as part of a team and unsupervised. I'm moving to the area and thought this role would be ideal.

Later

Interviewer: Would you give me an example of where you have been under a lot of pressure at work and how you have dealt with it?

You: Yes, at Zipperco we often had very tight manufacturing deadlines and a lot of the team would be quite stressed. I would take time to listen to each member of my team and by remaining enthusiastic [positive and cheerful] this would reassure them and we always managed to have happy customers who said they liked the Zipperco customer service, remained loyal, and spent more with us year on year.

Later

Interviewer: Digital Widget is very different from Zipperco, do you think you can adapt?

You: There are some fundamentals in manufacturing environments, but you are right, there are also differences. However, dealing with customers cheerfully is the same anywhere. I have a positive approach to change both personally and in business and I'm keen to learn, which means you won't be spending a lot of time and money while I get up to speed.

Later

Interviewer: Well, that's all from me, is there anything you'd like to add?

You: Only that you'll find me positive and cheerful and my customer service experience in manufacturing will mean we can start getting results very quickly.

You can see in each answer we have mentioned or alluded to being cheerful and positive, we mention manufacturing and we highlight benefits—loyal customers who spend more, saving money, and getting results. And while it may be obvious that a happy team is good for business, we have explained the benefit.

Ideally the interviewer will make a note saying: Positive, cheerful, hit the ground running.

We have also done something that is a good technique. In our replies we said: 'while I get up to speed' and '…we can start getting results very quickly'. We don't say 'you wouldn't' or 'we could', we assume that this is going to happen. Doing this helps the interviewer imagine you in the role. This is what sales professionals call the assumptive approach.

Conclusion

In this chapter you have learnt how to craft the key message you want to get across at the interview. You understand:

- Why you need a key message or personal statement
- How to create a key message using the job advert or person spec
- Features, advantages, and benefits (FAB)
- How to ensure the interviewer(s) remembers your key message

***

Now that you have a clear message, is there anything lurking online that can undermine you? We'll address that in the following chapter.

5 Cleaning up Your Online Reputation

The way to gain a good reputation is to endeavour to be what you desire to appear.

Socrates

Depending which figures you read, anywhere between 60% and 90% of employers will check your social media accounts prior to the interview. In this chapter you will learn:

- How to identify what interviewers might be looking for
- How to deal immediately with any 'bad press'
- How to build a good online reputation

If you don't use social media, jump to the section 'building an online reputation'.

What are employers looking for?

Everybody has a past. Depending how much you use social media your past may be all over these platforms: the good, the bad, and the ugly.

Employers and recruitment consultants want to be sure of three things: first, that the information they have from you is correct; second, that there are no skeletons, scandals or major contradictions; third, they will be looking for supporting information that might strengthen an application.

Correct information predominantly relates to your LinkedIn (or if you are in Germany Xing) account. Does the information match that on the CV or application form? If you have said you are keen to work in Artificial Intelligence (AI), is that reflected in your account? Are you a member of AI groups? Have you written an article on AI?

Skeletons and scandals will mostly likely stem from Facebook, Twitter and Instagram. You don't need me to tell you what may be considered appropriate or inappropriate by a recruiter. There may be, of course, grey areas. Whilst in most countries freedom of expression is perfectly acceptable, recruiters also have a right to interpret what is said, expressly or otherwise. So strongly held beliefs of any persuasion could set alarm bells ringing.

Finally, a recruiter may well find information that supports and strengthens an application. You may have competed in a sport, raised funds for a charity or completed a challenge that shows you in a good light.

Ask yourself what you would look for.

Action to take immediately

Google yourself, with certain variations like your name, your town or region. If nothing comes up that is fine, but if anything comes up you need to plan how to address it. If it is in any way controversial a measured response is required. If positive it will work to your advantage and if embarrassing, again, a considered response.

Ensure your LinkedIn profile matches the CVs you are sending out. Check if it is too biased towards a particular type of role or industry and if you can make it more general. Turn off the feature that 'announces' any changes you have made. Add a post or two that might support your key message.

If your Facebook and Instagram pages generally reflect you partying and being boisterous, half-dressed or if you are sharing strongly held political or other views that some might find difficult, I suggest you use the privacy settings to confine who can see your account. Scan Twitter for any tweets that might come back to bite you and remove them. If you are desperate to remain a keyboard warrior with controversial views, you may want to run your account anonymously—in fact, most keyboard warriors don't use their own identity.

How to build a good online reputation

Your professional profile will sell you to potential employers and headhunters looking for a particular person—whilst that is another book altogether, it's worth touching on it here as it really can support your application.

If you are particularly keen to work in, say, manufacturing customer services, sharing articles about the subject, writing articles, initially on your LinkedIn page or on a blog platform like Medium, will allow you to be found when recruiters google your name. It doesn't have to be Pulitzer Prize winning, just enough to demonstrate your competence.

Submitting articles to organisations for blogs can work well. My local chamber of commerce is always looking for content, so you don't need to be in the national press to surface.

If you are raising money for charity or taking part in a challenge—and by the way, if you have not or don't plan to, it's worth considering—make sure the local or regional press is aware.

The advantage of having some content out there is that when recruiters google you there's a fair chance they will come across your articles. An additional benefit is that if there is any content on the internet that may be embarrassing, adding additional content will help push it down in ranking.

Conclusion

In this short chapter we have learnt that between 60% and 90% of employers will check your social media accounts prior to an interview. You now understand:

- What recruiters are looking for when they do
- How to tidy up your online profile
- How to build a good online reputation

***

You're making good progress. Now that you know when your interview is, what do you need to do to prepare for this specific interview?

6 Preparation

Whenever you are asked if you can do a job, tell 'em, 'Certainly I can!' Then get busy and find out how to do it.

Theodore Roosevelt

In this chapter, you will learn about preparing for an interview. You will be shown:

- How to do research on the company
- How to know every detail of your CV and personal statement
- The importance of preparing questions
- Why you need to practise answering questions
- Planning your route
- What to take

This is where we get in to the nitty gritty. You've been told the company would like to interview you and in a week's time you will make your way to their offices and meet them face to face. How are you going to prepare?

Research

One of the first questions in interviews is 'What do you know about us?' This is not necessarily designed to test your knowledge, but to gauge how much they need to tell you. Either way, it is a good idea to find out more about the company to demonstrate interest, enthusiasm and to provide opportunities to ask questions.

The obvious starting point is their website. Read all you can and make notes of any questions you have. In particular what their news or social media channels are saying. Google the company and scan any news stories. Try to keep any research broadly around the company you will be working at rather than the parent company or operations in other territories. Make a note of cultural tone. What are they proud of, what are their marketing messages? This will provide you with an opportunity to be empathetic in the interview.

Keep your questions positive unless there is something you really want to dig in to. For example, you might ask: *'I notice you had a fun day and raised money for charity, do you do that every year, and may all employees get involved?'* or *'You have a number of operations around the world, do you have much to do with each other, or are you fairly autonomous?'* If something really bothers you about what you have found, do raise it: *'The press mentions you were sued for negligence by a former employee, could you tell me about that?'*

Be careful though, I went to a small company and they asked me what I knew about them. Having done mountains of research I said that I knew they were owned by an Indonesian bank. *'Are we?'* they asked each other. No one in the room knew and they sent someone out to find out if they were. Half an hour later someone returned saying: *'He's right, you know. Apparently, our parent company was sold six months ago.'* It distracted from the interview and, frankly, wasn't relevant.

Make sure you research the people who will be interviewing you. In the previous chapter, we established that a large number of recruiters will research you, so we are going to do the same. The reason for this is so that you can get a feeling for them before the face-to-face meeting. It might be so you can subtly hook into common ground. The interviewer may love playing football and if you do too, you can drop this in. They might have visited somewhere that you have been. Take advantage of common ground. If you are unsure of who will be interviewing you, call the company to find out—as we have said before, this shows you are interested in the application, doing your research and are planning ahead—all good traits in any employee.

There is the possibility your research uncovers something so damning

that you are not sure if you want to go to the interview. In this it
I suggest calling the organisation with your concern.

Type up a single sheet of paper with the key data you have gathered and any questions you have.

Visit the location where you will be working so that you know the way and have a look at the people coming and going: What do they look like? What are they wearing? What do they carry? Don't spend too long doing this, you may get arrested for stalking!

Knowing your resume/CV and relating it

I can't tell you how many people I have interviewed that don't know their CVs. Whilst using a CV or resume writing service is not a bad idea, not knowing what has been written is unforgivable.

This activity will fill you with more confidence than almost any other in this book. When you know that there is nothing you can be asked about on your resume that you cannot answer positively, your confidence levels will shoot through the ceiling!

This involves going through the CV or application form (you did keep a copy didn't you?) you sent in, and forensically stepping through it to first, be able to ask any question relating to it and, second, relate it to the vacancy.

Taking the scenario we have looked at, we'll give a few examples.

We'll look at asking specific questions in a later chapter, but using these questions to help us, we need to come up with positive responses for everything:

- Who
- Where
- When
- How
- Why

It starts with the personal statement, ask yourself who else says you are positive and cheerful. Why is this a benefit to the company? Do this with every statement in this section. When have you worked unsupervised? What do you like about manufacturing?

Go through each previous job, why did you leave? What did you like or dislike about the role—be positive, even if the answer is negative, for example: *'The only thing that was challenging was my manager could be abrasive and would sometimes say hurtful things. But she was under a lot of pressure and I learnt that this is not the way I would deal with staff.'* Demonstrating learning from negatives is a powerful way of showing self-awareness and remaining positive.

Some interviewers like to turn a positive into a negative, for example: *'Your CV says you were employee of the month in April 2018, why was it only that month?'* Look at everything you have stated and ask how it could be twisted and produce a positive reply.

Knowing the route to the interview location

The last thing you need on the day of your interview is to arrive late, get held up or, worse, get lost. The interview location may not be at the same place where you will work if successful, so make sure you plan your route. If you have time actually do it. If you cannot, use Google maps to view the route and location.

Give yourself time and arrive 10 minutes earlier as it may take a few minutes to get through security or sign in.

Getting your clothes ready

In the next chapter, we discuss what to wear to an interview. Make sure the clothes you want to wear are ready in advance. If you have established that a white shirt is important, you don't want to find it's in the wash basket when you are getting ready. Maybe have a spare top ready.

This may seem obvious but being well prepared in advance will give you a chance to clear your mind and relax.

What to take to the interview

Most people going to meetings take papers or a notebook, so it is absolutely right that you do the same. You are going to take your CV and the sheet of notes and questions you have drawn up. Put them in a transparent folder so that you can read them during the interview without extracting reams of paper and potentially dropping them. Take the person spec, job description and any other paperwork they have provided in the folder. Take a couple of pens so you can take notes. Wear a watch and keep your phone in case they want to call you but switch it off for the interview.

If the interviewer asks you to bring anything with you, for goodness sakes take it! In fact, if you do call them to ask who will be interviewing, or when you are told about the interview, ask if you need to bring anything… and do!

Most employees will walk around a building with a notepad, so by doing the same you will fit in. You will look 'ready for business' rather than carrying a briefcase or nothing at all.

And yes, this applies universally, whether you are going for a waiting job or a CEO role.

You might also want to take some examples of your work. Certainly, if you are a designer or produce visual work, a portfolio would be sensible. As a writer or web designer, making sure you have easy access to work is sensible.

Even if your work is not that shareable, you may have contributed to the company blog or have examples of online reviews where you were name checked.

Conclusion

If you carry out all the tasks in this chapter you will be superbly prepared, relaxed and ready.

You now understand:

- How and why to do research on the company
- How to prepare questions
- The importance and technique for knowing every detail of your CV and personal statement
- Planning your route and preparing clothes
- What to take to the interview

***

Now that you know what to prepare, the question is: *'What should I wear?'*

7 Presentation and Dressing for an Interview

*Elegance is not standing out;
but being remembered.*

Giorgio Armani

This chapter will explain how to approach what to wear and how to present yourself for an interview. You will learn about:

- The halo effect
- How to work out what to wear
- What to take to an interview
- The importance of personal hygiene

The halo effect

Have you ever looked at someone and drawn a conclusion about where they come from, what they do and what they are like? Of course you have. We all do it and it is called the halo effect, and no matter how open-minded we are, it has an effect on how we view people.

Your job, when entering the room and coming face to face with an interviewer, is to reduce any negative halo and highlight the positive.

For that reason, we need to dress appropriately, ensure we are well presented, and our personal hygiene is second to none.

And yes, once you get the job you can express your wacky side more, but not in the interview.

How to work out what to wear

In the previous chapter, we suggested visiting the work location and we mentioned observing what people wear and what they look like. Whilst respecting you as an individual, it is important to fit in, to be part of the team, to be an ambassador for your employer. So, if everyone at the workplace wears formal business wear with sharp haircuts, turning up to the interview in leather trousers, a t-shirt and a baseball cap may not hit the right tone. Equally, if you are applying for a job in a very trendy design agency or fashion house, a corporate business approach may not work—I was once told a candidate I had put forward looked too corporate.

The important thing to do is play safe and be appropriate—good life advice!

Remember though, you are not going to a party, wedding or on a date, you are going to a business meeting.

The importance of personal hygiene

As obvious as it seems, having neat, well-cut hair and clean clothes and shoes is going to work in your favour.

And it's amazing how many people do come into an interview looking unkempt and unwashed.

We have already said you are not going on a date, so strong perfumes and colognes are a no-no. This is a business meeting. Make sure you use a deodorant—and if you are against sprays and roll-ons, there are perfectly good natural deodorants available on the market—use one.

Try not to smoke and avoid eating garlic, onions or strong foods the night before. Use a mouthwash either way.

Because tackling the issue of personal hygiene is always a bit awkward for a manager and employer, and they will not want to upset the existing team, if this is an issue during the interview it will put a firm block on your application.

Conclusion

In this chapter, we have looked at how to approach what to wear and how to present yourself for an interview. You now understand:

- The halo effect
- How to decide what to wear
- What to take to an interview
- The importance of personal hygiene

***

In the next chapter, we'll look at how to get the edge using non-verbal communication and techniques for sounding just right.

8 Body Language and Speech

The most important thing in communications is hearing what isn't said.

Pete Drucker

This chapter will teach you the basics of positive body language, the importance of good posture and using language to give you an advantage in the interview. You will learn about:

- Open body language
- Posture
- Eye contact
- Relationship with the space
- Mirroring
- Complimenting and name-dropping
- The power of silence

Much of this chapter will come naturally to you—don't overthink it and use it as a checklist to ensure you have all the bases covered.

There is a lot of research to suggest that positive body language contributes a great deal to how people view what you are trying to communicate. Equally, the words we use and how we use them will have a dramatic effect.

We want to give ourselves an advantage, so we'll look at simple and easy techniques that can achieve this.

A firm handshake

I have three sons. If I have taught them nothing else (I hope I have!) it is the importance of a firm and confident handshake. Practise with a friend to ensure your handshake is not limp and weak or a painful vice-like grip.

Not every business culture shakes hands, and, in a post-Covid 19 world, some people will be understandably less comfortable with it.

I would take the advice given to people who meet royalty: only shake hands if it is offered.

Open body language

If I am talking to you with my arms folded and my legs crossed, you are probably going to think there is something wrong with me. And you'd be right. Open body language seeks to ensure that you appear at ease, positive and calm. Importantly, you will not be perceived as negative or defensive.

The best way to sit in an interview is in a neutral position. This means putting your hands on your knees and one leg slightly in front of the other. This gives the impression you are ready for action.

Do not fidget. Don't play with your ears or scratch your nose, both can imply you are not sure or, worse, not telling the truth—consciously avoid doing this by keeping your hands on your lap.

Avoid playing with your hair, this can imply attraction to the interviewer and while you may be attracted to them, this is neither the time nor place!

If you must scratch due to an itch, wait until the interviewer is speaking.

Posture

The Victorian Britons taught young ladies and gentlemen how to hold them themselves—deportment.

Good posture shows confidence and fitness. Bad posture makes you look downtrodden and weary.

What do we mean by good and bad posture? A bad posture would see your shoulders sloping forward, your back stooping, and your head hanging forward from your neck. In a good posture, your back will be straight or with an inward curve at the base of your spine (known as the lordosis), your head will be 'held high', shoulders back and chest out. This is worth practising as it is how your body is designed to be positioned and reduces aches, pains, and injury. Your ears should be above your shoulders and your shoulders above your hips.

A good exercise for 'resetting your shoulders' is to raise them up to your ears and let them flop after five seconds.

Avoid crossing your legs as it can look too casual.

Eye contact

Eye contact is very important in most societies. Many people find this difficult and I have heard feedback from interviewers saying: *'He had difficulty making eye contact.'*

The important thing to remember is to look at the person you are talking to, don't stare at them or fix on them. To avoid looking slightly scary, look naturally at their eyes scanning from one to the other and away when you are thinking. It's very important to look at them when they are speaking to you—again, by looking at one of their eyes then the other it will make you look natural and interested, nod in acknowledgement that you are taking in the information. Oh, and don't forget to take in the information!

When you are in a panel situation, always look at the person speaking to you. When replying, focus on whoever asked you the question and move from one panel member to the other starting with the questioner and returning to them when you are done.

Relationship with the space

When an actor is training, and when they prepare for a role, they examine the space they are performing in and ask what relationship the character would have with that space. For example, a prisoner may cower in the corner and be timid about the space, the space representing a jail cell. A celebrity or wealthy businessperson would own the space, swaggering around a penthouse. A priest may be respectful of the space representing a sacred symbol such as a church.

While this may seem a tad 'out there', it's worth thinking about your relationship with the room you are going to be in. Of course, it is unlikely you have ever seen it, but regardless of the size, grandeur or otherwise, you should think about how you relate to it. You want to appear confident, but not cocky, so when being invited to sit, move the chair a bit so that you are comfortable. That might mean pulling it back a bit or bringing it forward. Importantly, you are not going to cower or swagger!

Mirroring: physical

We often do this naturally when we get along with other people: they lean forward and you lean forward, they cross their legs and you cross your legs, you lean back and they lean back, you take a sip of your drink and so do they.

During some interviews, it's appropriate to mirror as it builds a bond. If you are both sitting at a table and the interviewer leans forward, you might lean in too. If they are leaning back with their feet on the table, I'd hold off.

Speaking

It's important to be clear and understood. We all have different accents and linguistic traits. Try not to rush when you speak. The Pinocchio effect suggests that people who are not telling the truth use more words to compensate; the sentence gets longer as they lie.

Avoid filling gaps with 'you know' and 'like.' These are simply words for *erm* and *um*. If you need to *um* and *err*, try silence. You'll need to practise this as the way we speak is so ingrained. Remember, you want to be understood and appear confident. If you speak a bit louder than you normally would, the *ums*, *ahs* and *you knows* tend to disappear. It will also compensate for a natural tendency to speak in a quieter tone when we are nervous.

Wait for the interviewer to finish a question before answering and never cut across or interrupt.

Mirroring: language and neurolinguistics

One technique used by negotiators is mirroring the last few words of a question to build rapport, gain more information, and/or confirm understanding. This is very powerful and simple to do.

The first scenario involves confirming information: *'If you are successful, how would you feel about meeting at our head office?'*

'If I'm successful a meeting at your head office would be absolutely fine' shows much better understanding than *'Sure, no problem.'*

The second scenario helps you get information, so in answer to the previous question you might say: *'A meeting at your head office?'*

'Yes, it would give us a chance for you to meet the board?'

'Meet the board?'

'Yes, they like to meet candidates before confirming appointments.'

'If I'm successful a meeting at your head office with the board would be absolutely fine.'

Of course, they may not reply like that, but it's a handy technique.

There's a theory that everyone has a dominant sense. Some are visual, some auditory, some kinaesthetic (touch) and some olfactory (taste and smell). Most of us enjoy great food, a beautiful scene, wonderful music, and the feeling of something soft to touch. This technique works by

63

listening to the words people use and mirroring them back. Here are a couple of examples:

Q: At Digital Widget our vision (visual) is to be market leader in 5 years' time. Can you see (visual) yourself putting in the work to help achieve that?

A: I can. It's always been my view (visual) that working hard pays off, so yes, I can definitely see (visual) myself helping you achieve the vision (visual).

Q: You may have heard (auditory) that we have a big conference every year and all staff and families attend. How does that sound (auditory) to you?

A: That sounds (auditory) great, it will really resonate (auditory) with my partner and children who love celebrations.

Q: We'll call (auditory) you about the next stage, if you are successful, how would you feel (kinaesthetic) about meeting at our head office?

A: If you get in touch (kinaesthetic) before the weekend, I should be able to arrange to do that, so no problem, I'll wait to hear (auditory) from you.

The key is to be natural, not to overdo it and be aware of the interviewer—I doubt that if you do this it will be a deciding factor in your interview, but it may well help you over the line.

Complimenting and name-dropping

Everyone wants to be liked and appreciated and, applied carefully, this knowledge can be used to your advantage. I say carefully because if done clumsily, you can come across as sycophantic and creepy. I have noticed in recent years that almost everybody being interviewed on TV or radio, says to the interviewer: *'That's a really good/important/interesting question.'* It is so common, you begin to wonder if the question really is good, important, or interesting.

During a job interview, unless the question really is a sidewinder, I would avoid saying a question is good, in large part because they wouldn't design the interview to ask dumb questions—even if some of them are!

Generic compliments like *'Digital Widget is clearly successful, and I'd love to be a part...'* or *'You have a very strong vision for...'* are fine.

Getting the interviewer talking is no bad thing, as long as you get all your messages across. I once said to an interviewer: *'You have clearly done well with the company, if I want to succeed here, what should I be doing?'* He spoke for a good 15-20 minutes about himself. I got the job and he later said to me how well I'd interviewed and how interesting I was; he'd done most of the talking.

I'd be wary of name-dropping. You want to get the job on your merits not on reflected glory. However, if a particularly proud moment in your life was receiving an award from a royal or a celebrity, that is fine, or if you know someone at the organisation in a senior role, you might mention that, but never imply that you are a better candidate by virtue of whom you know—unless the job is for a celebrity agency!

The power of silence

There is a danger when responding to a question or asking a question that if you either don't get a response to your answer, or an immediate response to your question, you start filling the silence with waffle—don't. Embrace the silence and learn to love it, it's never as long as it seems.

Here's an example:

Applicant: *'So, yes, I know I can hit the ground running and start generating extra sales.'*

Silence

Applicant: *'I mean, I may need training on the systems, but yes, we should be getting sales pretty much straight away...'*

Silence

Applicant: *'Obviously, there will be quiet periods, but that gives us a chance to look at improving systems…'*

Silence

Applicant: *'I'm sure the systems are fine, but…'* And so on.

It is far more powerful to end on silence, which would sound something like this:

Applicant: *'So, yes, I know I can hit the ground running and start generating extra sales.'*

Silence

More silence

Interviewer: *'Excellent, building sales is important to our growth plans.'*

As you can see, it is more powerful, and as we discovered earlier, we avoid the Pinocchio effect.

Conclusion

Much of the subject matter in this chapter is natural to most of us, but it is worth being aware of it so you can gain marginal advantages and avoid messing up your interview.

In this chapter, we have looked at the basics of positive body language, the importance of good posture and using language to give you an advantage in the interview. You now have a good understanding of:

- Open body language
- Posture
- Eye contact
- Relationship with the space
- Mirroring
- Complimenting and name-dropping
- The power of silence

***

The next two chapters dive into what interviews are really about.

9 How to Answer Interview Questions with Confidence Part 1

Does anyone have any questions for my answers?

Henry Kissinger

This chapter will identify the most common, and some less common types of interview questions, why they are being asked and how to approach them. The next chapter will provide an exhaustive list of questions for you to work through.

To get there you will learn:

- What lies behind interview questions
- The importance of being positive
- The STAR approach
- Classic tricky questions
- Trick questions and wind ups
- Gaps in your CV
- Role-plays
- Dealing with inappropriate questions
- Brain teasers

What lies behind interview questions?

As we identified in Chapter 1, the purpose of asking an applicant questions is to identify if they have the skills, experience, and aptitude for a particular role. When we examined the recruitment process, you'll remember a decision matrix was drawn up. The questions very simply allow the interviewer to identify if you do or do not meet the criteria, or at least to what extent.

It really is as simple as that. The interviewers will look at criteria such as having customer service experience and ask questions that will enlarge on the application.

Some questions are easily answered such as what were you doing for the months between these jobs, and some require behaviour-based questions such as *'Tell me about a time when you had too many things to do and you were required to prioritise your tasks.'*

The importance of being positive

In answering questions, it's vital to stay positive. We discussed in Chapter 6 that learning from a negative experience is a good way of making a situation positive.

Casting your mind back to Chapter 1 and putting yourself in the recruiter's shoes, ask yourself if you and your customers would like an employee who is generally positive or often has a negative outlook on their experiences.

For example, if you were asked what you disliked most about working in a bar, you could say: *'I hated cleaning the toilets at the end of a shift, it was awful, stinky, and I couldn't wait to leave that job.'*

A positive reply might be: *'We all had to take turns cleaning the toilets at the end of the night and, as you can imagine, it could be quite messy. But every job has the less fun bits and we all have to do our bit even if it's not a fun task.'*

The interviewer wouldn't want to do that task either, but it demonstrates your attitude and the first answer suggests the applicant is thin-skinned whereas the second one shows a positive attitude.

The STAR approach

While some questions simply require you to provide facts in a positive light, others are designed for you to provide evidence of certain behaviours. The STAR method helps you address those questions confidently.

S - *Situation*: Describe a specific situation. Give enough detail for the interviewer to understand. The situation can be from work, voluntary work, school, college or personal life. Ideally in that order.

T - *Task*: Describe what you were trying to achieve.

A - *Action*: Describe the actions you took.

R - *Result*: Describe the outcomes, even if the overall outcome was negative, highlight the positive aspects and learning.

Example: *'Tell me about an important written document you were required to complete?'*

Situation - When I was working with a local football club, the local council told us we needed to replace the toilets otherwise they would close us down.

Task - We needed to raise 10,000 very quickly and I was asked as treasurer to apply for a grant from the national football association.

The forms were quite complex and required a business plan outlining what we would do with the 10k.

Action - I prepared the document over a weekend and showed it to the treasurer of a local tennis club, who had made similar applications. She made some suggestions and we submitted the documentation.

Result - We received the funds, the toilets were replaced, and the club remained open. I think this was a result of remaining positive and being open to learning from others.

In the next chapter, you'll have the opportunity to answer a whole load of questions using the STAR approach.

Reframing and redirecting

The UK Prime Minister Tony Blair was a master at redirecting questions from interviewers. If he was asked *'What have you got to say about the Government's appalling record on supporting the widget industry?'* He would reply along the lines of *'The widget industry is, of course, very important to the UK economy, but the question we should be asking is what is being done for the economy as a whole, which of course the widget industry is a part of. And the answer is we have grown by x% which is record growth, and I am very proud of that.'*

I am not suggesting you are as bold as that, but if you are asked a question for which you don't have an exact answer, you can reframe or redirect the answer to one that you do. For example: *'Tell us about an award or prize you have won at work.'* Now, you may not have won any prizes or awards at work, not least because not all employers do that, so you might reframe it to *'My last employer didn't give awards or prizes, but one of my best achievements was developing the customer program and this was highlighted in the company newsletter by the CEO.'*

Classic tricky questions

There are questions that always turn up and some people struggle with. You might be tempted to use humour to brush over them, but I would urge caution as it can appear to be flippant, or worse, inappropriate:

Q: *'What are your weaknesses?'*

A: *'A whole lot of booze and waking up in strange places.'*

Tell us about yourself

The opening tricky question is *'Tell us about yourself.'* We have discussed this in Chapter 4. At a minimum, the personal statement on its own would do, but I suggest adding pertinent information about your career. Using the job application, you could say: *'I studied business and art at college and my first job was in a cafe. It taught me a lot of the fundamentals of customer service and I enjoyed working in a good team, which is probably why I spent two years there. I'd always wanted to travel, so I spent a year in Europe and the Middle East, working as a volunteer at various children's charities. This taught me to manage myself and my time. When I came back, I worked on a temporary contract for a marketing company, which helped expand on my business diploma. Now I am working for Zipperco in customer services. In summary, I'm a positive and cheerful customer service manager with experience in the manufacturing sector who can work as part of a team and unsupervised.'*

Don't share personal details that are irrelevant to the job. Some interviewers may be interested in where you were born and what school you went to aged 6, but they are hardly relevant. Prepare an answer to this question remembering that everything you say can be questioned.

Gaps in your CV

There's nothing wrong with taking time out, but some interviewers get twitchy about gaps in your work history, so it pays to have a positive explanation for each gap. It might be that you couldn't find a job for 3 months or you were depressed and couldn't get it together. My advice is to talk the gaps up rather than being defensive. In the case of job searching something like *'I came to the end of the contract and wanted some time to reflect on what I really wanted while I looked for another job, I was in no rush'* could work well.

In the case of illness, while there is no shame in having times when you cannot cope (I have been there!) most interviews are not the time to wave a flag about it. Try something along the lines of *'It had been quite stressful working at XYZ Company and after I left I needed to think about where I really wanted to go, I learnt that it's important to take time out, to reflect, and take stock.'* This last answer does not deny problems but frames them positively. And that is what we are aiming to do.

With the increase in popularity of 'gig' jobs, gaps in CVs are much more explainable; a series of casual and temporary jobs is not uncommon for most people not set on a career path.

What can you bring us?

I was once interviewed for a sales role where I was asked this. I replied that I was hardworking and enthusiastic, and they said: *'Good, but what can you **bring** us?'* I replied that I was a team player, would hit the ground running and had experience in their sector. I didn't get the job and when I asked Dave, a friend of mine who had been in sales for many years, he said: *'Ideally they wanted you to bring the customer database from your existing company and at worse a couple of existing customers.'* Now, I am not saying that everyone who asks that question is after the same thing, but oftentimes it is looking for something you have or have access to that they don't. That may be knowledge of how to set up a proven digital marketing campaign or access to the buyers at target customers. Have a think about what you could bring to the company that they may not already have.

I would have been stealing if I had taken the customer database to a new job, so ensure that a) it is legal and b) if you are unsure, check your existing contract. You might then say: *'Well, it would be illegal to give you the customer database and I would never steal from an employer. My contract forbids me from approaching existing customers for six months. After that, though, I can.'*

Strengths and weaknesses

For most people, the strengths question is fairly straightforward - keep it relevant to the CV and application rather than personal.

It's the weaknesses that trip most people up. I once asked a young woman what her weaknesses were. She replied that she loved partying at the weekend and was always hungover on Mondays. Slightly taken aback at her honesty, but to a degree respecting it, I asked if working Saturday and taking Sunday and Monday off would allow her to party and recover, should she get the job. She thought for a moment and said: *'Probably not, I'd most likely be hungover on Tuesday morning.'* The point is, be honest, but not that honest!

The main reason for asking this is not to understand your weaknesses, but to understand first, how self-aware you are, second how you manage and deal with it and third what you have learnt from it.

The most clichéd reply is *'I tend to work too hard'* to get the recruiter to think *'Great!'* Remember, it's about how self-aware you are. I'll give you an example in my case: I am quite dogmatic. If I have an idea or theory, I believe is right, I can be quite forceful with it. Some might describe it as being passionate. I do understand this and will try to ask other people their thoughts first. Oftentimes, this will allow me to adapt my theory or idea and it turns out better. For example, I thought in one job that the reception people who answered the phones should have some knowledge about the products we sold as when customers came through, they would say no-one at reception seemed to know about what we did. I asked others their view in a management meeting and we wound up ensuring all employees knew about our products and services, which resulted in more sales and salespeople and customer service staff dealing with important issues rather than general enquiries.

Have a think about your weaknesses and how you deal with them and importantly, have an example ready. It can really stump you when you happily answer the question but cannot give a practical answer—think STAR!

What would other people say about you?

As part of being self-aware, why not ask friends and colleagues what they think your strengths and weaknesses are. It will help you answer this question at an interview. A great answer is *'Well, I actually asked some friends about this and they said…'*

Dealing with the 'awkward' situation

A question often asked of managers in retail and customer-facing roles is:

'You have a member of staff who has quite strong body odour. How do you deal with it?'

What the interviewer is looking for is your ability to tackle issues head-on and not prevaricate. The awkward situation stems from the fact that there will be some offence caused. No getting away from it.

A good answer might be: *'It's important to deal with the issue and not let it drift. I would contact HR and take advice. Subject to that, I would meet the employee telling them I have an awkward issue to discuss and if they are happy for me to do that. I would explain that there is an odour around them that may be off-putting to some customers and members of staff. I would explain that it may be their clothes or something else, but are they aware of it? I would then gain their agreement in resolving the issue and reassure them that they are a valued employee.'*

It's always a good idea in organisations where there are support services such as HR, finance, marketing, facilities and so on, to use them to help make decisions. That way any negative reaction will not backfire on you.

The important thing is how you approach the situation. It's worth considering scenarios where you have had to deal with a similar predicament.

Role-play

Role-plays can be awkward if you are not used to them. The best approach if you know you may have to do one is to practise with a friend or family member. If that's not possible, play it through in your mind.

You will most likely be asked to play out a scenario typical to the role. It is likely then, that you will have been in the situation or something similar. A sales role might require a sales situation, customer service an awkward customer, and a management role a difficult staff situation.

Either way, it is worth taking a couple of notes out of the actor's playbook and that is to try to get in the zone by transporting yourself to a real situation and 'acting' as if you were there. Imagine the room is a real setting and detach yourself temporarily from the interview.

Remember, this is not a test of how well you can perform as a thespian, but of how you can apply your experience and aptitude to a 'real' situation.

Control questions

These questions seek to find out if the answers you give in relation to activities or events outside work are congruent with the work-related questions. For example, let's say you gave the impression you were a team player, preferring to work with others, very sociable and love working. Then you were asked what you would do with a lottery win and you said, buy a desert island so I can be on my own. Or your favourite childhood memory is sitting alone on a hill watching the world below you. These answers might be counter to the initial impression given. Try to make sure they are aligned or acknowledge the counterpoint to demonstrate self-awareness.

Trick questions and wind-ups

In theory and if you are well prepared, there should be no such thing as a trick question as you know why questions are being asked. But there may be times when a question is asked where you are not sure, for example: *'If you were to join us, would you be able to bring the customer database from your current company?'* The question you have to ask yourself is do they want you to steal or do they want to see if you are the sort of person who would steal. I hope your response would be tactfully honest: *'Well, you are either asking to steal or you want to see if I'm the sort of person who would steal. But the answer is no, I would not break the law for an employer.'*

It may be more nuanced than that though, so you have to think, why are they asking this question? And if need be, put it back to them.

We've established that recruiters will ask behaviour questions to identify if you have the aptitude for a role, but some recruiters will use aggravating questions to gauge your response. Rather than asking how you deal with rude people, they might actually be rude to you to see how you react. As a recruitment consultant, I have sent candidates to interviews where this has happened. They have been upset and left the interview. When I have fed this back to the client, they have said they were testing the client under stress. While this may work in the military, I don't personally hold with unplanned role-play for civilian jobs, but it does happen, so be aware.

If this does happen, keep your cool, don't fight back, be dignified and ask yourself what they are trying to test here. Are they trying to make me lose my temper, be rude, snap?

In genuine conflict situations and in these unannounced role-plays, the mirroring techniques we discussed in the previous chapter can be of great use. Keep your body neutral and look interested:

Interviewer: This is all rubbish?

You: Rubbish?

Interviewer: Yes, working with children, I bet you were partying the whole time!

You: Partying?

Interviewer: Yeah, getting drunk and dancing.

You: Dancing?

Interviewer: Yeah, I bet it was one big party while you travelled. What have you got to say about it?

You: Say about it?

And so on. In genuine conflict situations it allows information to be gathered from the antagonist and time to understand why they are upset. When you are ready you can reverse the question flow and label it with something like:

'It sounds like you are feeling angry about something?'

'What is making you feel this way?'

'What's making you feel that this is rubbish?'

If you really are pressed for an answer, present hard facts:

'I worked with children for 4 days out of seven and did tourist trips on two days. For the other day I would relax and read and yes, there were weekly social gatherings involving drinking and dancing.'

If an interviewer wants to test responses, a role-play is much more appropriate as, done clumsily, the wind-up can lead to inappropriate questions and statements.

Dealing with inappropriate questions

Thankfully, these occurrences are mercifully rare, but they can crop up, sometimes because of the character of the interviewer and sometimes inadvertently.

Discriminatory questions are generally asked of one candidate and not of all. For example, when a candidate is asked what their spouse feels about them working may be inappropriate if only women are asked that question, but not if the role involves long periods of travel and all candidates are asked. So a woman candidate being asked *'How does your partner feel about you taking this job?'* may be inappropriate, whereas *'Many people in relationships have found the travelling hard and left after a few weeks, how do you feel your relationship would cope?'* asked of all candidates would be OK.

When a question is asked along these lines it can be tricky. First because if you want the job, you may not want to 'rock the boat', but also it is intolerable to be subject of any discrimination.

There's also the danger of seeing discrimination where it does not exist. For example, if the question about partners is asked of all candidates to address an existing concern.

So, how do you respond if it does happen? I would repeat the question back to give the interviewer a chance to expand. For example: *'How does your family feel about you taking this job?'* You might reply: *'How does my family feel?'* Whether or not it is discriminatory will depend on the answer. *'Yes, in the past families have found it very hard to have a parent away for so long at a time, we ask all potential employees as it can be such a major issue.'* would be OK as opposed to *'Yes, as a mother it could be hard for you to be away from your children and they may well miss you.*

To an extent, we all discriminate every day many times. We make unfounded judgments about people's appearance (the halo effect in Chapter 7) and make decisions about who we engage with or not. Where the wrong occurs is where a decision to not confer a benefit is made because of that discrimination.

If having given the interviewer the chance to explain themselves you are convinced the question is inappropriately going down a discriminatory path, you might a) ask yourself if you want you want to work for a company that operates like this and b) establish the degree of harm being done. I would ask the following question and note the answers:

Is this a question you ask all candidates, and will it be a deciding factor in my application? Depending on the answer, the outcome of the interview and the jurisdiction will inform what you do next.

Inappropriate comments might be purely offensive. Offence is not always intended on transmission but is defined by how it is received. I can be offended by comments made about women, disabled, or gay people because although I am neither a woman, disabled nor gay, I don't want to be thought of as being complicit with the interviewer in sharing those views. While the rights of the interviewer to hold and share those views are beyond the scope of this book, the point is they are inappropriate to share in an interview. If this did happen to me, I may be very tempted to write to the company and express my displeasure at the comments.

If an interviewer does start making comments you find offensive, I would politely say that you find them inappropriate. There is a chance that they are trying to see what your reaction is as we discussed earlier, so you should respond firmly and with dignity. This is the correct response either way. If the interviewer does not desist, politely leave and write to the head of HR or a senior person in the organisation explaining what happened.

Brain teasers

1. Why are manhole covers round?
2. If you have a 5-litre jug and a 3-litre jug, how do you accurately measure 4 litres?
3. How many golf balls can you get in a Boeing 747?
4. Name 3 uses for a house brick other than building.

Some companies ask questions that examine your approach and creativity when solving a problem that may or may not be answerable.

If you are going for a highly sought-after job in a cool company, or an organisation where the standard of education amongst employees is very high, you may well be asked these types of questions. If you are seeking an admin job in a bank or a customer service job in manufacturing, it is less likely.

The secret to answering these is to practise doing them using brain teasers found on the internet and in books. Like IQ-type tests, they exercise that way of thinking and lateral approach to solving problems. If you do take the time to practise these, it will do you no harm if you are not asked these questions!

And the answers to the questions?

1. Manhole covers are round so they don't fall into the hole.
2. The jugs
   - Fill the 3-litre jug and pour it in to the empty 5-litre jug.
   - Re-fill the 3-litre jug and add what you can (2 litres) to the 5-litre jug.
   - That should leave 1 litre in the 3-litre jug.
   - Empty the 5-litre jug and pour the 1 litre into it.
   - Fill the 3-litre jug and add it to the 1 litre in the 5-litre jug.
   - You now have 4 litres.
3. Golf balls and 747: Here's my approach that I would say out loud so they hear my thinking: '*I don't know the diameter of a golf ball, so if I cannot google it to find out, I am going to assume it is around 3cm. I also don't know the internal volume and dimensions of a 747, and it would depend which model, but I could probably get that from Boeing if I could go online. Guessing the width of a...*' And so on, the point is I am thinking it through and acknowledging I need extra resources.
4. Brick - This is to check creativity, so off the top of my head: paperweight, door stop, exercise weight, smartphone stand. Not very original. What would you say?

Conclusion

We have covered a lot in this chapter. Some interviews will cover much of what is discussed, and some will be a chat over a coffee and barely touch it, but now you are prepared.

You now understand:

- What lies behind different types of interview questions
- The importance of being positive
- The STAR approach to behaviour questions
- How to approach some classic tricky questions
- What to do with trick questions and wind-ups
- How to address gaps in your CV
- How to deal with inappropriate questions
- The purpose of brain teasers

***

You have taken a lot in. Well done. Next we'll apply it and you'll ace any interview whilst gaining greater self-awareness and confidence.

10 How to Answer Interview Questions with Confidence Part 2

The more I practice, the luckier I get.

Arnold Palmer

In this chapter, we will apply much of the learning from the previous chapters by answering an array of interview questions. I guarantee that if you can answer all the questions positively, you will be able to answer almost any interview question.

As you work your way through them, take time to think and hone your answer. If you get stuck, think about situations other than work and how they might apply. Many answers will be the same or very similar and it's good to be consistent and say to an interviewer: *'As I said when you asked be about…'*

In most cases, you know the answer, you have just never thought about it before. Now is chance to think about it rather than during the interview.

I have included notes on the question in italics and some examples.

Remember, stay positive, relevant, and know you may be questioned on your answer. Let's do it.

Questions:

You

1. Tell me about yourself
   Self-awareness and background – use personal statement.
2. How would you describe yourself?
   Self-awareness and background – use personal statement.
3. What makes you unique?
   It's difficult to say without knowing the other candidates. You could state that and ask what they think based on the applications. Re-state personal statement. Have something you believe is unique to you.

Them

4. What do you know about our company?
   Checking research and preparedness.
5. What do you know about our industry sector?
   Checking level of knowledge and experience.
6. Who are our competitors?
   Checking research and industry knowledge.
7. What is the name of our CEO/MD?
   Checking research and preparedness.
8. Why is our company of interest to you?
   Checking motivation and expectations – use as an opportunity to gently flatter.
9. Why do you want to work for us?
   Checking motivation and expectations – use as an opportunity to gently flatter.
10. What can you bring to our company?
    Are there any unique traits such as industry contacts or knowledge that they don't already have and to add to their existing strengths?
11. Why are you interested in this position?
    Checking motivation and expectations – use as an opportunity to gently flatter.

Why you?

12. What skills would you bring to the job?

Looking for existing skills you have and any extras they do not.

13. Why are you the right person for this job?
    I will say 'I don't know what the other candidates are like, and that will be your decision, but I'm...'

14. What makes you different you from our other candidates?
    I will say 'I don't know what the other candidates are like, and that will be your decision, but I'm...' You might also have unique experience in your sector or industry.

15. Why should we give you this job?
    I would turn this back and say: 'Because you think I'm the best candidate, if you don't you shouldn't give me the job'. Add qualities from the key message.

16. Are you overqualified for this role?
    Checking to see if you might get bored and your motivation. 'I'd rather fly with an overqualified pilot than an underqualified one!'

17. Are you willing to travel?
    May have had difficulties with previous staff. Be honest with yourself and them.

18. Would you be willing to work nights and weekends?
    Checking flexibility.

Your relationship with work

19. How long would you expect to work for this company?
    Checking career aspirations and motivation.

20. Why do you want to leave your current job?
    Checking career aspirations, motivation, commitment, and to uncover any issues. Never speak ill of previous employers, be positive whatever the situation: 'I have had some great experiences, but I think I can be more productive elsewhere.'

21. What will you do if you don't get this job?
    Checking career aspirations and motivation. Remember desperate is not attractive, but keen is fine and having options looks good.

22. Why are you changing careers?
    Checking career aspirations, motivation, commitment, and to uncover any issues.

23. What do you like most about your current job?
    Checking motivation and attitude.

24. What do you like least about your current job?
    Checking motivation and attitude – be positive and show what you have learnt.
25. Can you walk us through your CV?
    Similar to 'tell us about yourself.'
26. Can you explain these gaps in your CV?
    Want to be sure you were doing something constructive.
27. Explain why you've had so many jobs?
    Concerned you might leave quickly – be positive; you wanted broad experience, circumstances, but now it's time to focus all that experience on one job.
28. What do you do in your spare time?
    Checking that there is more to you than meets the eye and ensuring hobbies and interests are not all consuming to the point they affect your job.
29. Your CV says you are interested in [name of interest], when did you last do this?
    Many people put reading, or a sport they haven't played for years as an interest – this question checks that it is a genuine interest and digs in to find out more.
30. What is your dream job?
    Focus on the qualities of the job: 'One where I can quickly start delivering results, work happily with great colleagues, where I learn and develop and there's a sense of common purpose and we are all successful.'
31. What is the best job you ever had?
    Again, focus on the job qualities and environment.
32. When were you most satisfied in a previous job?
    Be positive – looking for motivation. 'When we were all delivering results/working well/ nailing the project.'
33. Describe your perfect company.
    Again, be positive: 'One where everyone is delivering results, and we are all working happily.'

Self-awareness

34. What are some positive things your last manager would say about you?
    Seeking self-awareness. If you had an appraisal refer to that.

35. What is one negative thing your last boss would say about you?
Again, refer to an appraisal if available. Be selective and show learning.
36. How would your friends describe you?
Seeking self-awareness – why not ask friends and you can give a very honest reply!
37. What adjectives would your friends use to describe you?
Seeking self-awareness – ask your friends.
38. Do you have a mentor?
If not, you might point to self-help books or any learning you do.
39. What are your greatest strengths?
See the previous chapter – be honest based on what you think and people have told you. Keep it work-related.
40. What are your weaknesses?
See the previous chapter and demonstrate awareness and learning.
41. What do you like most about yourself?
Similar to strengths and weaknesses.
42. What are your greatest achievements?
It is worth throwing in a personal and work achievement. Align it to your personal statement.
43. What are you most proud of in your life?
Similar to previous question.
44. What's the most embarrassing thing that has happened to you?
Seeking to find out how you cope in certain situations. Be honest but selective! Show learning.
45. What was your greatest failure, and what did you learn from it?
Many organisations now take the view that failure shows you are innovating. We learn from failure. Use STAR.
46. What's the biggest lesson you've learnt from a mistake you've made?
As above.
47. What is your least favourite thing about yourself?
Keep this work-related, not physical. I would like straighter teeth, but that has nothing to do with work. Reframe to a weakness.

48. What is your biggest regret and why?
   My stock answer is: 'I don't really have regrets. I cannot control the past so there's no point worrying about it. There are certainly things I would change if I could have my time again…' then I'll give an example.

49. What makes you uncomfortable?
   Keep it work-related. E.g. It might be when colleagues are upset or angry. Not when someone is too close on a train. Use STAR.

50. What is your greatest fear?
   Keep it work-related.

51. What are your life goals?
   It may be to join a circus and travel the world, but for an office-based job, or working on a construction site, it's worth aligning it to the interviewer's needs – 'To be a life-long learner, happy, productive, and appreciated for as long as I can'.

52. Who or what has had the greatest impact on your career?
   Aimed at seeking out motivation and learning.

53. How would you define success?
   Are you aligned with their goals? Use your research.

54. How do you want to improve yourself in the upcoming year?
   Are you invested in self-improvement? Show it.

55. Do you have a personal mission statement?
   Time to write one!

Motivation & style

56. How many hours per week do you normally work?
   Part of this is about how well you manage your time and the other is about commitment – show balance.

57. Do you ever take your work home with you?
   As the previous question – 'I try to make sure all work is done during work hours, but inevitably there are occasions when the job demands an extra mile. So yes, but not if I can help it.' Use STAR from the previous chapter.

58. What three things are most important to you in your job?
   Motivations. Your choice, but NOT: Money, holiday allowance and gym membership. Rather, feeling valued, being part of a successful team etc. Be prepared for a follow-up – 'How do you know you are valued?'

59. What will you miss about your previous job?

Seeking motivation and attitude. Be positive, but not sentimental.

60. Do you prefer to work alone or on a team?
    Demonstrate flexibility. By all means state a preference, but not one that is counter to the requirements of the job. 'I like being part of a team, but I'm happy to get my head down and work alone when needed.'

61. Do you find it difficult to adapt to new situations?
    Identifying if you'll fit in quickly and adapt when there is change. Be positive, use the STAR method.

62. What is your ideal working environment?
    Will you fit in?

63. What are you pet peeves about work colleagues?
    To understand you more. Be honest and show how you deal with it using STAR.

64. Are you a morning person?
    Will you be difficult to work with? Can you get up, will you be late?

65. What motivates you?
    Obviously, this will vary, but keep it work-focussed: 'being part of a good team', 'bringing in the big deals', 'looking at a day's work and knowing I've done a good job.'

66. How do you stay motivated?
    When the going gets tough, how do you cope? Use STAR.

67. How do you keep yourself organised?
    Explain if you have a system, and if it helps, see Chapter 12 and the in-tray exercises.

68. How do you prioritise your work?

    As above.

69. How do you handle conflict at work?
    Do you avoid or deal with it? Always best to deal with it. Use STAR in your example.

70. How do you work under pressure?
    Similar to how you keep motivated.

71. What are your passions?
    Try and keep it work-related. So, you may say: 'Well, I love playing the guitar, but in a work setting…'

72. Who are your heroes?

This can depend on the industry or role. In fashion, it might be a designer, in management a certain leader. Whoever you choose, think about why.

73. If you could be anyone else, who would it be?
    I was told at an interview that my answer 'I don't have any desire to be anyone else, I am happy being me' was a great answer. I followed it up by saying I would like the experiences of some other people, but not to be them. The key to this lies in why you might want to be someone else.

74. Are you more of a leader or a follower?
    Every employee has to be both, to some extent. Reframe.

75. What was the last project you managed and what was the outcome?
    Use STAR.

76. Describe your work style.
    This is seeking alignment with the needs of the job – adapt personal statement.

77. What is your management style?
    As above.

78. What qualities make a good manager?
    This may relate to you or how you like to be managed.

79. What qualities make a good leader?
    As above.

The future

80. Where do you see yourself in 5 and or 10 years' time?
    To see if you plan to stick around. Keep it work-related.

81. How much do you expect to earn in 5 years?
    'What I am worth.' Be ambitious, but realistic.

82. What are your salary expectations?
    Don't sell yourself short. If you are the right person for the job, they will pay the going rate. You don't want to work for a company that employs the wrong person because they are cheaper!

83. What would you do if we offered you this position and your current employer offered you more than we are to keep you?
    Read the section on counteroffers in Chapter 16.

Control questions

84. What is your favourite film/movie and why?
    Trying to get to know you – align with other answers or acknowledge difference.

85. Name three skills or traits you wish you had.
    To see what you are doing about acquiring them.

86. If you could have a superpower, what would it be and why?
    Trying to get to know you – align with other answers or acknowledge difference.

87. Describe a favourite memory from your childhood.
    As above.

88. What is your favourite website and why?
    As above.

89. What was the last book you read?
    This is a factual answer. Be sure you remember what the book is about. If it was a long time ago, google a synopsis.

90. What is a book that everyone should read and why?
    Trying to get to know you – align with other answers or acknowledge difference.

91. What commonly accepted view do you disagree with and why?
    As above.

92. What good causes are you passionate about?
    As above.

93. If you won a big lottery prize, would you still work?
    Motivation and alignment.

94. What questions haven't we asked you?
    Having prepared to answer so many questions, you can pick one that you feel you have a great answer for.

Behaviour questions – Use STAR

95. Describe a situation where you used persuasion to convince someone to see things your way.

96. Describe a time when you were faced with a stressful situation that demonstrated your ability to cope.

97. Give me a specific example of a time when you used good

judgment and logic in solving a problem.

98. Give me an example of a time when you set a goal and were able to meet or achieve it.
99. Tell me about a time when you had to use your presentation skills to influence someone's opinion.
100. Give me a specific example of a time when you had to conform to a policy with which you did not agree.
101. Discuss an important written document you were required to complete.
102. Tell me about a time when you had to go above and beyond the call of duty to get a job done.
103. Tell me about a time when you had too many things to do and you were required to prioritise your tasks.
104. Give me an example of a time when you had to make a split-second decision.
105. What is your typical way of dealing with conflict? Give me an example.
106. Tell me about a time you were able to successfully deal with another person even when that individual may not have personally liked you (or vice versa).
107. Tell me about a difficult decision you've made in the last year.
108. Give me an example of a time when you tried to accomplish something and failed.
109. Give me an example of when you showed initiative and took the lead.
110. Tell me about a recent situation in which you had to deal with a very upset customer or colleague.
111. Give me an example of a time when you have motivated others.
112. Tell me about a time when you delegated a project effectively.
113. Give me an example of a time when you used research skills to solve a problem.

114. Tell me about a time when you missed an obvious solution to a problem.
115. Describe a time when you anticipated potential problems and developed preventive measures.
116. Tell me about a time when you were forced to make an unpopular decision.
117. Describe a time when you set your sights too high (or too low).

You will certainly not be asked all these questions—I hope. But if you can confidently and positively answer them, I promise you will not only be able to ace any interview but will also know a lot more about yourself. You will have much greater self-awareness and confidence. Make sure to review them and keep practising.

Conclusion

In this chapter, you have practised answering over 100 of the most frequently asked questions at job interviews. You now:

- Know more about yourself
- Can answer almost any question thrown at you
- Are nearly ready to go and crush that interview

***

You are on the home straight now, but first you need to prepare the questions you will ask the interviewer. And these can propel you forward dramatically.

11 How to Ask Great Questions in Interviews

*It is not the answer that enlightens,
but the question.*

Eugene Ionesco

This chapter will help you work up a few questions to ask at the interview. You will learn:

- How to use questions to demonstrate suitability and interest
- How to use questions to cement your message
- How to overcome possible objections
- How to get more information, be active

I have successfully used the following simple questions and techniques in job interviews, sales pitches, and bids for multi-million-pound contracts. They are very simple and have a huge impact. If you remember nothing else from this book, you will remember and use these for the rest of your life.

Let's backtrack a bit first. I am often asked, should I ask questions at an interview? What should I ask? Obviously, the answer is yes. But some people when asked if they have any questions meekly say, *'No, I think you've answered everything.'*

Asking questions shows you are interested, you were listening, and you prepared—all good traits!

Demonstrating suitability and interest

There will be a number of practical questions you have such as how much training there will be, when you might start, how much holiday allowance there is.

It's important to not ask questions just for you, such as salary, benefits, and leave. You should have a couple of curiosity questions that may have arisen during research in Chapter 6. For example, the company may have been family-owned and sold and you want to know if they are still involved or, whether this branch has much to do with other branches.

Write these down and you can ask them when invited. What often happens is the questions are answered during the interview, so when asked you can check your notes and say: *'Well, I had questions about training and start dates which you've covered and you mentioned that you work closely with other branches—out of curiosity, I know the family sold the company six months ago, are they still involved?'*

You can then move on to the first genius question.

Genius 1: cementing your application

You want the interviewers to be reminded of why they chose to interview you, and it will help you if you know why so you can build on those strengths. The question that will draw this out is:

'What was it about my CV and application that made you want to interview me?'

This is a great question because it gets the interviewer(s) to say out loud what they like about you. It also allows you to understand what to build on.

I try and ask this at the beginning of the interview. So, they might ask a question early on such as 'tell us about yourself' and at the end you can pop the question.

In a sales presentation or pitch I will kick off by saying: *'Before I start, may I just go around the room and ask what it was you liked about the initial proposal?'* You might be able to ask it during the small talk phase:

'Well, you found us OK then?'

'Yes thanks, and I appreciate you asking me to see you, I'm very excited about this role—I'm curious, what was it about my CV and application that made you want to interview me?'

'We liked your positive approach and the fact you have experience in manufacturing and dealing with the public. We're thinking of opening a business to consumer offering next year and it could be useful.'

If you don't feel you have the opportunity to ask it earlier, you can save it for later. Make sure to reinforce what they say: *'I'm pleased about that, I am positive and do enjoy the manufacturing sector, so I am glad that came across—the B2C offering sounds very interesting!'*

But always make sure you ask this question, if for no other reason than to get feedback from which you can learn.

Be active, but not too active!

Asking questions during the interview shows you are listening and interested. You can seek clarification and use the opportunity to reinforce your qualities: *'You said that sometimes everyone has to go the extra mile to hit a deadline. I'm used to working weekends and occasionally pulled an all-nighter to get the job done, how often do you find yourselves in that position?'*

But too many questions will make you sound like you are not listening and a bit slow on the uptake. I mentioned earlier in Chapter 8 that it can be good to get an interviewer talking, but don't force it.

I once had a candidate who had obviously been told to get the interviewer talking and after a while I had to firmly say: *'I am very keen to find out as much as possible about you to assess your suitability for the role, if we are not careful we'll only know about me.'*

Genius 2: overcoming objections

Imagine getting a call like this after the interview: *'We really like your application, and it was very close, but we had an applicant who had more experience of business to consumer so unfortunately we won't be offering you the job.'*

What if business to consumer was something you did have experience of, but you had played it down as you didn't think it was that important for this role?

Not all recruiters are perfect, situations change between when job descriptions are drawn up and interviews take place, and not all are good communicators. But it's too late now, the job has gone, and you are kicking yourself—if only I'd known about the business to consumer need!

The way to mitigate this is with the following question:

'Is there anything you have heard or haven't heard that gives you any doubt about my suitability for this role?'

I have used it in job interviews and countless sales meetings, and it has saved me many times. The interviewer will tell you what you need to know to tackle any objections there and then. Oftentimes, they will repeat your positive attributes:

'I don't think so, you are positive and cheerful, you have a good attitude and great experience. I suppose the one area is business to consumer as we may well branch into that in a year's time and we don't see much experience there.'

This is your chance to swoop in and crush the misunderstanding. *'I see, well at Zipperco we sold direct to the public and I helped set up the customer journeys, so I had a couple of years B2C experience from set-up to dealing with customer issues.'*

Now, you may find that the objection is difficult to overcome, at which point you need to establish how import it really is: *'Although my B2C experience is limited, I am a consumer, so know full well what it's like from the customer's point of view. Is this a deal-breaker, or a nice-to-have?'*

'It's probably a nice-to-have, but it would be useful.'

'Well, I am sure I can rise to the challenge, I'm positive, keen to learn, and sympathetic to consumer needs, being one myself!'

Always ask this question. It demonstrates a desire to learn and, importantly, will stop you needing to kick yourself down the line.

What next?

It's good to be clear about what happens after the interview. If you have not been told what the next steps are, find out. That way you can check progress appropriately after the interview.

Conclusion

You know that you will ask a number of questions to fill in any gaps, but the two questions you have to ask are:

'What was it about my CV and application that made you want to interview me?'

'Is there anything you have heard or haven't heard that gives you any doubt about my suitability for this role?'

In this chapter you have learnt:

- To demonstrate suitability and interest
- Cement your message
- To be active, but not too active
- To overcome possible objections

♦ ♦ ♦

Question-and-answer interviews are not the only selection tool. How are you going to comfortably approach selection tests and presentations?

12 Being Brilliant at Selection Tests and Presentations

After a long time of practicing, our work will become natural, skilful, swift, and steady.

Bruce Lee

Question-and-answer interviews are not the only selection tool. We'll now look at understanding:

- The importance of practising tests to get into the zone
- How to approach an in-tray exercise
- How to tackle a presentation
- What could happen at selection days and assessment centres

Not all recruiters carry out tests, but when they do it is vital you read all the instructions and the whole question before attempting to answer. There are numerous cases of points being dropped by getting the question the wrong way around—read it twice.

Some tests and tasks are designed to check your listening skills and ability to follow instructions. A famous one is where there is a detailed instruction and the last line says: *No points will be awarded for completion of this task. Points will be awarded if you disregard it.*

When preparing a presentation, read the brief thoroughly.

Skills tests

Skills tests are designed to check if you can do what you say you can to the standard required by the company.

Depending on the vacancy, this could vary from creating a word document and performing a mail-merge, writing some JavaScript, fitting a tool into a lathe or dismantling a gun. The job description will be clear about the skills you need so make sure you practise them.

In the case of software, you can google 'most commonly performed tasks in [name of software]' or 'essential [software] skills'. Make sure you are up to speed on the software. If you don't have it, try a free trial and failing that follow videos and free tutorials.

If you will be required and you have said you can program a router or mix a perfect cement, make sure you can and at the very least go through the process mentally to be sure you have not missed any steps—visualise yourself getting it spot-on.

All skills have varying degrees of proficiency and requirements for a job. You could use a word processing package every day of your working life and never perform a mail-merge. You could use a spreadsheet every day and never need a Vlookup or work as a mechanic on Harley Davidsons and never a Honda. It pays to find out to what extent and in what areas you will be tested—give them a call.

Make sure you are up to speed on the skills required.

Numerical, verbal, and logical reasoning

The best way to approach these tests is to get in the mindset. This means practising tests of this type. There are a number of providers of these tests and if you can find out which provider's test you will be doing, it will help with preparation.

Your options vary from signing up to an online test preparation service, to buying books on the subject and googling free tests you can do.

Whichever you choose, your goal is to get comfortable with the way of thinking these tests are aiming to test.

Aptitude and psychometric tests

These tests—and, in reality, test is the wrong word as they are more evaluations or assessments—are the hardest to prepare for as they are identifying personality traits and aptitudes. It's quite possible that you could successfully be performing a particular role for many years for which you do not have a natural aptitude.

Most of these assessments have control questions that flag if you are saying what you want the test to hear for a particular trait.

I would be wary of trying to 'game' these types of assessments.

In-tray exercise

The in-tray exercise aims to see how you cope under pressure and, more importantly, how you prioritise your work.

Faced with a certain amount of time and a pile of jobs that need doing, you may be interrupted during the exercise with another job or 'emergency'. It is unlikely you will be able to do them all in the time given.

You may be a natural at this and/or very good at managing your time, but here's an approach to deal with it.

You'll create four piles (or virtual piles if on computer) and divide the tasks amongst the four. They are:

1. **Urgent and important** - there is an imminent deadline and it is important (e.g. Do payroll figures before tomorrow. Ship new order by Friday. Put out fire). These are jobs that need action first.

2. **Important, not urgent** - e.g. Ensure all customers are aware of new support service launching in three months. Get new computer for new starter in a month. These jobs need planning.

3. **Urgent, not important** - These tend to be interruptions or a meeting you don't need to be at. These jobs can be delegated or avoided.
4. **Not urgent, not important** - Junk mail, distraction such as social media. These can be ignored.

When you get an interruption, your job is to work out which pile it should sit in and act accordingly.

If you haven't figured it out already, order the work, then start with what you must do and then plan.

If you haven't already, start using this approach to plan your workload—either at home or work or both, so you get in the groove. It's also a great answer to the question, 'How do you prioritise your work?'

Presentations

Many people get very worried about speaking in public—we'll talk about nerves in the next chapter—but the key to success in public speaking is preparation.

Your first task is to read the brief thoroughly and be absolutely clear about how long you have. It is fine to finish under the time you have, but not to overrun.

One of the greatest speakers of the 20th century was Winston Churchill. He wrote every word of his speeches. He said he spent an hour working on every minute of a speech he made.

If you have ever seen a TED Talk—and if you haven't, I highly recommend you do—many TED speakers spend up to 100 hours preparing their talks, which might only last for fifteen minutes.

Now, I am not suggesting anything like that amount of time to prepare. However, prepare and practise you must.

Here is a simple approach that will help you give a good presentation:

1. **What is the purpose of the presentation?** Is it to share figures and draw conclusions? To present an idea? To

propose a change?

2. **Kick off with a question**: Why are we beating sales targets but still struggling? Could we increase productivity with more home-working? (tell them what you are going to tell them)

3. **Answer the question** with circa 3 supporting answers (tell them)

    - Use a **quotation**
    - Use a **statistic** - make sure you keep the source to hand
    - Use an industry **resource**

4. Offer a **counter-argument**

5. **Shoot it down**

6. **Restate** key points

7. **Good last line** - answer the question

Typical interview presentation topics can vary from 'sell yourself' to 'launch a new product or service' or can be more role-specific such as marketing, finance, or operations.

I'll give an example of how I would approach this for a three to five-minute talk about a proposed new service: WaaS or Widgets as a Service.

Purpose: To persuade senior management we should be launching a cloud-based widget service.

Why would customers want a cloud-based widget service?

The answer lies in three key areas. But before we address them, let us consider some statistics from the International Widget Makers Association. Adoption of cloud-based services by widget users has increased by over 20% every year for the past three years.

So why would clients want a cloud-based widget service? First, for mobility. In 2014 Eric Schmidt, CEO of Google, proclaimed: 'The trend has been that mobile was winning. It's now won.' Several years on, the widget industry stays stubbornly in the 20th century. Our customers have changed and are changing by 20% every year.

Second, flexibility. With fluctuations in widget service demand at different times of the year, widget service users don't want to be paying for capacity they are not using. Hence, they often switch suppliers during this time of year to reduce costs. Using a WaaS model, they can dial the service up or down according to their needs, saving them money and time spent moving to another provider.

The third reason is far greater reliability and security. A report last year on CIO concerns showed that their biggest concern was security followed by keeping the wheels turning. A well-designed WaaS solution takes care of all those worries.

Now, there are those who will say the monthly cost of a service like this ends up costing more than the existing approach. And they'd be right. But only partly: When you factor in the capital costs of hardware, the cost of maintenance and the cost of downtime, not to mention the lost opportunities of not being mobile, there is no doubt a cloud-based approach wins hands-down.

This presents a huge opportunity for Digital Widget. With more loyal customers who are more successful our future growth is secure.

Our customers are already moving to cloud in other parts of their business, they want more mobility through mobile access, they want flexibility of supply to save them money and they want security and reliability for peace of mind.

That's why customers want a cloud-based widget system. That's why we should provide a WaaS offering. Thank you.

Presented at a measured pace, the example above took me three minutes to present. Three tips to help you:

1. Count to four to yourself before each new paragraph
2. Count to two after each full-stop (unless there is a new para and see above)
3. Highlight the words you want to stress

If you think you are presenting too slowly, you are probably just about right, if a little fast. You need to give your audience time for the words to sink in, to have impact.

Whatever you prepare, make sure you can support it and have sources.

An interviewer, in the above case, might ask:

How old is the data from the International Widget Makers Association?

A: It's from an article in last month's newsletter.

What would the costs be for us to implement this?

A: Part of identifying the size of the opportunity is to establish the capital and running costs before our competition does (don't know basically).

What was the report on CIO concerns? Widget CIOs can be quite old-fashioned.

A: It came from the latest Gartner global CIO survey.

As an interviewee, you may need to wander into the realms of role-play. The key thing is to back up what you are claiming and to acknowledge if more information is needed.

Slides

You may have heard the phrase *'Death by PowerPoint'*. This is the type of presentation that involves dozens of slides and a presenter who monotonously reads from them. Worst of all, he or she reaches a point where they'll say: *'Well, I don't need to read the whole slide to you.'*

The golden rules then are: NEVER read from the slide. The only time you refer to a slide is if it is data or an image and you are presenting an analysis.

The reason is your audience can read faster than you can present. So, if your slide lists five reasons employees should have new hardware this year, we have already got it before you have started speaking about number one.

If you must include slides with all the information, do not reveal the content until after you have presented them.

The best presentations do not rely on slides. First, because if the technology fails—and it does—you may not be able to use them anyway and second, if your audience is partially sighted, they are irrelevant.

I say that from bitter experience. I once presented to a retail billionaire. I'd spent hours preparing persuasive slides and had five minutes to present. My laptop still hadn't booted after two and he just said: *'Just tell me what you want and what's in it for me?'*

I took slides to a presentation I was to give for an exam, and one of the examiners was blind. Don't rely on slides.

Notes

Use notes—break them into sections and highlight, or format so they are alternately indented; this will help you keep your place. Churchill did this.

Cards work but can be dropped and shuffled so number them clearly. I often use a piece of A4 or letter-sized paper and fold it in 3. This gives me 6 'panels'.

Hold the paper or cards flat. While it doesn't matter if they are seen, it will reduce the visual impact of the cards to your audience.

Practise and repeat

Practise, practise, practise. Say the presentation out loud and time it. If you are overrunning, cut it down, but don't speak faster. If you are underrunning, don't worry but maybe slow down your presentation.

It's very useful to present to a friend or family and ask them for feedback. Take the feedback, then present again until it is really good.

The great thing about repeating and repeating is you become less reliant on the notes and the presentation becomes ingrained and more natural.

Did I say you need to practise it?

Selection days and assessment centres

Selection days and assessment centres can span multiple days and involve almost everything this book has covered or be a couple of hours having a test and an interview.

By bringing together groups of people, recruiters can see how you interact with others by giving groups certain tasks.

Often called problem-solving, the classic mistake made by young managers, is to assume it is an opportunity to show how assertive they can be and how good they are at solving problems. The true aim is to show how you make best use of your team to tackle the problem.

So, a typical task might have a group of six people. The task is not that important as the goal is not to complete the task, but to identify the approach taken by the candidates. A 'leader' might be assigned and if that is you, the best approach is to kick off by going around the group saying something like this: *'OK, we have 20 minutes for this task, let's take five minutes to get views from each of us and we'll see where that takes us.'* Make sure to praise each person's input and sum up.

If there is no leader, someone may jump in first with something like: *'Right, what we need to do is break into two groups and come up with two solutions and we can pick one.'* Make sure you praise the input and bring the group's view back to the equation: *'That's a great suggestion, shall we first take 4-5 minutes and get everyone's view on how we should approach this?'* Even if that is not adopted the observers will see you value the team.

The key point to note is that these selection days are not to knock out the other applicants, but to show how well you work with and in a team.

You are being watched

Selection days and assessment centres may also observe you in a social setting, so be careful how you behave when you think the formalities are over. A number of companies, and the military, will tell you the day is over and provide a lavish meal, flowing drinks, and a free bar so everyone can get to know each other. The observation here is to see if you can behave diplomatically.

An extension of this is to either abruptly stop the fun or wake everyone up at 2 am and get them to complete a task. You have been warned!

Conclusion

In this chapter, you have learnt about preparing for tests, presentations, and assessment centres.

If there are two key messages, they are: read the question or brief and practise.

Specifically, you should now be brilliant and know:

- The importance of practising tests to get into the zone
- How to approach an in-tray exercise
- How to tackle a presentation
- About what could happen at selection days and assessment centres

***

You should be very well prepared now, but what can you do if you feel anxious or nervous about being interviewed?

13 Beat Interview Nerves and Jitters

One important key to success is self-confidence. An important key to self-confidence is preparation.

Arthur Ashe

In this chapter, you will learn how to reduce interview anxiety. Specifically, you will learn:

- That the more prepared you are, the better you will feel
- Not to pin all your hopes on one job
- To visualise success
- That you are going to a business meeting not an interrogation
- That exercise reduces stress
- To eat and drink well and get a good night's sleep
- Some nervousness is better than overconfidence

I play in a band. I'm the lead singer and we do a few gigs here and there. For the first two or three years I had the words to the songs in a blue folder. I didn't really need it, but it was there, on a stand in case I lost my way. If I didn't have it, I would panic and rush around trying to find it. Before each gig I would stand in the shower asking myself why I was putting myself through this, why did I feel sick and panicky? What if it all went wrong? What is they don't like us?

The truth was, while I was quite prepared, I wasn't fully prepared.

My way around this was to learn all the songs properly over a period of a month. I knew most of them anyway, I just had to commit them to memory—that was back in 2008 and now I know the lyrics, the chords and arrangements of over 60 songs. That's about three hours' worth of music and words. I occasionally rehearse them mentally and might look up a lyric I think I am misquoting.

Now I don't need the blue book, the only nerves I get are of excitement and wanting it to go well. I am confident I know what I am doing, because I do.

The secret to dealing with nerves is preparation. That's what this whole book is about: understanding the recruitment process, preparing and then taking action.

I've put this at the end because you should be fairly well equipped by now. However, if you still feel worried, here are some tips that should help.

Do not pin all your hopes on a particular job

The perfect job quite often isn't. A friend studied art at university, and you'd think the ideal job would be working in a national gallery. She did. She got the job and it was riddled with office politics and boring.

One of the interview questions you will have prepared for is *'What will you do if you do not get this job?'* Noting that 'desperate is not attractive', having other options is important for you and shows the employer you have choices and are not dependent on them—it makes you more desirable.

Visualise the meeting going really well

Most top sportspeople walk through their performance in their minds prior to a match or contest.

In the days before the interview, visualise yourself performing really well and being happy and relaxed. If negative images sneak in, make them really small, remove the colour from them and return to the positive images and make them big and colourful.

Meditation can help greatly with this, or self-hypnosis. There are a number of apps and books on these subjects that can be helpful.

Remember this is a meeting not an interrogation

Would you be nervous if you were meeting a colleague to discuss a future project? Probably not. The interview is as much for you to get information as it is for the employer. You should know that some interviewers get very nervous and are often unprepared.

If you suffer from sweaty palms, take a handkerchief or tissue with you to face-to-face interviews where you will need to shake hands.

Make sure you are in good shape

If you are physically well, it will help you mentally. For a week before the interview, if you don't already, get some exercise to get the heart going: scientists have found that regular participation in aerobic exercise can decrease the overall levels of tension, lift your mood, improve sleep, and improve your self-esteem.

If you are reading this the day before the interview and you don't exercise frequently, about five minutes of aerobic exercise can begin to stimulate anti-anxiety effects. So, go for a 30-minute walk and clear your head.

Food and drink

Do not drink alcohol the night before the interview. I like a drink now and then, but I always wake up in the middle of the night if I've had a few. Not good before an interview. Similarly, lay off the caffeine the afternoon and evening before and go easy on the morning of the interview.

Don't eat any strong or rich foods the night before—first, you don't want to smell of onions or garlic [see personal hygiene in Chapter 7] and second, you don't want to risk bringing on an unsettled stomach. Play safe.

Prepare your clothes and kit

Make sure the clothes you are going to wear are ready and laid out the night before; have a back-up plan if you spill something on a blouse or shirt by having a spare clean and ironed.

Put all your paperwork in a clear folder and make sure it's ready to hand over to your interviewer.

Go to bed in good time

Earlier than normal if possible and try to get a good night's sleep. If you have difficulty nodding off, try some deep breathing exercises: breathe slowly in for a count of 10 and out for 10, do these 10 times concentrating on your breath.

On the day

Get up in good time so that you are not rushing. I suggest taking the day off work, if you can, so you are not worried about getting caught in meetings or out of the workplace.

Have a stretch and do some light exercise. Eat a light breakfast, drink water, and avoid a second cup of coffee if you like your caffeine fix. Make sure you stay hydrated up until the interview; you will feel better and your voice won't sound dry or croaky.

You should now be prepared and have tackled your nerves as far as possible. One final though on nerves: it's good to feel some level of nervousness, it shows you are taking it seriously. Much better than being overconfident and coming across as arrogant and under-prepared at the interview.

Conclusion

In this chapter, you have learnt about minimising the feelings of anxiety and worry about your interview. You have learnt:

- That the more prepared you are, the better you will feel
- Not to pin all your hopes on one job
- To visualise success

- That you are going to a business meeting not an interrogation
- That exercise reduces stress
- To eat and drink well and get a good night's sleep
- Some nervousness is better than overconfidence

***

Before and after the interview you can still affect the outcome. How? We'll look at that in the next chapter.

14 Communicating Before, During, and After the Interview Process

One person with passion is better than forty people merely interested.

E. M. Forster

This chapter will help you get all the information you need whilst leaving a positive impression with the recruiter. You will learn:

- When and how to request information
- How to leave the right impression
- What not to do

I have sat in a number of interviews where the candidate didn't know something they could quite have easily asked in advance. I have also sat in offices where a colleague has shared a good update from an applicant with the rest of the team. Equally, I have also had candidates that were never off my back in a slightly creepy way!

Getting information

Much of this book is about preparation and knowing what recruiters want generally and specifically. This requires information and the more the better.

The best approach is to do as much analysis as possible at each stage, drawing up a list of questions that need asking.

- Before applying to gauge the strictness of a particular need: *'You have asked for two years' experience, would you consider 18 months?'*
- Before interviews to clarify the structure or format: *'You have said someone else will be in the interview, is it someone I should be aware of?'* or *'You have said I'll be doing some tests, what sort of tests are they?'*

This information can be gathered by telephoning the recruiter or agency handling the vacancy. If there is an agency, NEVER circumvent them by going directly to the client company.

If you do not need to know anything extra to prepare, no need to call.

Leaving the right impression

Before each interview, I suggest dropping an email confirming your attendance and understanding of details—it's a professional thing to do, and not many people will do this. Something like this:

Dear [contact name],

I am writing to confirm that I will attend the interview for the role of [job title] at [time] on the [date] at [location] with [name of interviewer].

Many thanks for your help setting this up, and I look forward to the interview.

Kind regards,

[your name]

Write it in your own style, don't duplicate at each stage, don't waffle, but acknowledge the contact's help and confirm your understanding—simple.

If the person the message is going to is the recruiter, it will leave a good starting impression and if it is an agency or administrator, there's a fair chance they will highlight that you are a keen and professional candidate.

After each interview, I will pop an email to the interviewer or agent that says thank you and highlights very briefly any points of clarification that came from the questions asked at the end of the interview.

I have had these emails ready to go and added detail before sending them about a couple of hours after the interview. Do not send the email as you leave the building!

You may address it directly, or ask the agent or administrator to pass it on:

Dear [contact name],

Thank you very much for meeting to discuss the [job title] position at [company].

I enjoyed the interview and after finding out more about [company] still feel positive about the role.

I sensed some concern from your colleague [name] that I didn't have much experience at [whatever it is] and would like to reassure you that I am a quick learner and always keen to embrace better ways of working.

I look forward to meeting you again if I am successful in getting to the next stage of interviews.

Kind regards,

[your name]

Don't be sycophantic or sound desperate, just dignified and professional.

There is of course the possibility that after the interview you are not keen on the vacancy, either because the role is not what you thought it might be or because of something inappropriate said during the interview. In that case, you can withdraw the application:

Dear [contact name],

Thank you very much for meeting to discuss the [job title] position at [company].

After hearing more about the role, I am not sure that I would be the best candidate, the advertisement said some travel, but every week would be too much. For that reason, I would like to withdraw my application.

Thank you again for your time and I hope you are successful in recruiting for the role.

Kind regards,

[your name]

This is very professional and courteous.

Communications with agencies are generally done via phone, so this information will likely be conveyed that way, but an email clarifying it is not wasted and puts on record the situation.

Agencies

Some years ago, when I worked for an agency, a candidate applied for a sought-after job. He was pinning his hopes on it and chased me several times a day by phone and in person to see if he had been chosen for an interview. The role involved sales and I described him as, amongst other traits, 'tenacious'.

He did get an interview and continued to chase me about the result. It's worth pointing out here that one of the reasons companies use recruitment agencies is to deal with this side of the process. I explained that I would call him as soon as I heard anything as if he was successful, I would get my commission, so clearly I was motivated!

I did get a call a couple of days later from the client, but not the one I expected—the candidate had called them directly to find out the result. The result was he didn't get the job because a) he didn't respect business etiquette and b) he was too pushy. The company also highlighted that they weren't sure if I was adding value as it was my job to 'weed out' applicants like this.

I mentioned the story to another recruitment friend, and he described the candidate and said he'd had him do similar things—this results in a perfectly keen candidate effectively alienating agencies who can help him.

The point of this story is NEVER circumvent the agency.

The flipside of annoying a recruitment consultant is being a good candidate, so communicate, be straightforward and respectful, and you should remain front of mind for all the right reasons.

Chasing up—keep it brief

The opposite of leaving a good impression is a bad one as the last story illustrates. Desperate is not attractive and if someone is always being interrupted by a phone call asking what's happening, it can get irritating.

But you have a right to know what is going on. Having established at the end of an interview what happens next, it's fine to hold them to it. So, a call that might go: *'Hello Al, it's [your name] here, you interviewed me for the [job title] role and said you'd let me know by the 20th. That was yesterday and I'm very keen to find out if I am still in the running.'*

Just don't call every day.

Conclusion

In this chapter, you have learnt how to get all the information you need whilst leaving a positive impression with the recruiter. You now know:

- When and how to request information
- How to leave the right impression
- What not to do

***

You now have the tools to pass the ultimate interview—let's put it all together in the next chapter.

15 Putting It All Together The Big Day

Real happiness lies in the completion of work using your own brains and skills.

Soichiro Honda

Wow, you've come a long way in a short time. You should be proud of yourself.

In this chapter, we will pull together all you have learnt, first in a brief visualisation and second on a checklist.

The visualisation will help you see and experience success whilst reinforcing the learning. The checklist will make sure you have all the bases covered in a logical sequence.

The big day

Today is the day you have your interview. Last night you went for a 30-minute walk, had a light supper and after putting out your interview clothes went to bed earlier than usual. You relaxed and visualised a successful interview and have had a good night's sleep.

This morning you did some light stretches when you woke up, washed, used a deodorant and had a light breakfast and a glass of water. You got dressed after breakfast to avoid any spillages!

Your interview is at 10am, so you have an hour to get there, though it's only half an hour away. You take your folder with notes, CV and paperwork and leave the house at 9. When you arrive at the bus stop, the bus is full and you have to wait for the next one, which is in ten minutes time—it doesn't matter because you have lots of spare time.

You hop off the bus and are a 5-minute walk from the office. You make your way there arriving with 15 minutes to spare. You check through your CV and notes, you walk around the block to kill a few minutes and then go to reception and say you are there for the interview.

You are taken to the seating area in the reception and offered a coffee. You ask for a glass of water instead. While you have a few minutes, you breathe deeply ten times. You are feeling a bit nervous, but you know this is natural and you are also confident you know what you are doing.

The interviewer comes out and as he approaches you stand and smile shaking hands firmly in response to an outstretched hand while maintaining eye contact. The interviewer takes you into a room, you look around it and take it in and take the seat you are offered. You sit up straight, shoulders back, one foot slightly in front of the other.

Introductions are made, there is another person whom you would report to, and you are given some information about the company and the job—you ask if you can take some notes.

You are then asked, *'Tell me about yourself.'* You give a natural answer that touches all the points. At the end you say: *'What was it about my CV that made you want to interview me?'* You are told that is a good question and they answer providing useful information that you can build on.

The questions come and go and there are none you have not prepared for. You have to reframe and redirect a couple of them, but you answer confidently.

It's your turn to ask some questions. You tell them they have covered a couple you prepared earlier and ask for clarification on a couple of points. Then you say: *'You mentioned earlier you wanted to interview me because of my experience and achievements. We have spoken for around 35 minutes. Is there anything you have, or have not heard that puts you in any doubt about my suitability for the role?'*

The interviewers look at each other, they know this is a good question, the manager says: *'No, I think it was a very strong interview, we'll let you know the result by tomorrow as we'd like to start making offers next week.'*

You ask when next week and are told by Wednesday.

You say: *'Thank you very much, it sounds very interesting and having met you, I'm still very enthusiastic about the role.'*

On the way you home, you think about what went well and what could have been better and on balance you are very pleased—you know you couldn't have done much better.

When you get home, you send an email to the recruiter saying you enjoyed meeting them both, you are still keen on the role and look forward to hearing from them by Wednesday.

And that is it. You have done everything you can and it's a question of waiting, you can do nothing more. You can only control the controllable and that's what you have done.

Interview checklists

The following two checklists are: first, a 'pre-flight' checklist to keep you on track and second, an after-interview checklist to give you focus for learning and improvement.

Interview checklist for...	✓
I have a copy of the job advert and have analysed it [c.1]	
I have a copy of the job specification and have analysed it [c.1]	
I have a copy of the person spec and have analysed it [c.1]	
I have cleaned up my digital footprint [c.5]	
I have sent an email accepting and confirming interview details	

[c.14]	
I have written up and know my key statement [c.4]	
I have been through my CV and questioned every part [c.6]	
I have researched the company taking notes and questions [c.6]	
I have contacted the company with questions regarding the interview format if needed [c.14]	
I have practised answering questions that could be asked [c.9-10]	
I have prepared questions for the interview [c.11]	
I have made sure my skills are up to date [c.12]	
I have practised doing numeric and verbal reasoning tests [c.12]	
I have prepared and practised any presentations [c.12]	
I have recently had a haircut [c.7]	
I know where the interview is and how to get there [c.6]	
I have observed the workplace and know what sort of people work there and what they wear [c.6]	
I have chosen my clothes and they are clean and ready [c.6]	
I have my notes, paperwork and pens ready [c.6]	
I am getting exercise to reduce nerves and feel bright [c.13]	
I will get a good night's sleep before the interview [c.13]	

After-interview checklist

Activity	Yes	Not Sure	No
I arrived on time			
I was well presented			
I didn't smell of smoke, food, or body odour			
I maintained good eye contact			
My body language was open			
I was generally positive			
I managed to answer all the questions positively			
I answered all the questions relevantly			
I asked and know why they wanted to interview me			
I asked and know if there is anything they had or hadn't heard that put them in any doubt about my ability to do the job			
I know what happens next and when			
I sent an email thanking them for meeting me and stressing that I am still interested/not interested			

For any actions answered 'no' and 'not sure' ask yourself how you could improve and what you will do differently next time.

For those actions answered yes, well done!

Conclusion

In this chapter, you have studied a visualisation method to help you see and experience success whilst reinforcing your learning. You have the checklists to make sure you have all the bases covered in a logical sequence and you can reflect on your experience.

***

You are now at a point where you are ready to deal with the outcome of the interview—the offer of a new job or moving to the next stage. Or rejection.

16 Offer or Rejection

The more time you spend contemplating what you should have done... you lose valuable time planning what you can and will do.

Lil Wayne

What happens next?

The interviewers will discuss you straight after you leave. They will probably form a firm opinion—very strong candidate or, great experience, not sure it's a great fit with the team or, I'm a bit unsure, there's definitely something there. They will then need to compare all the candidates based on their input on to the decision matrix (see Chapter 1) along with any test results and decide whom to appoint or take to the next round.

If there is a next round of interviews, they will invite back everyone they think is in the frame. If they are going to appoint and there is a stand-out candidate, it is easy. But if they are aiming to appoint, and two candidates are neck and neck on the decision matrix, they might ask both to come back for another interview. A sort of tie-breaker.

Either way, you will either be accepted or rejected. Let's deal with rejection first.

Rejection

Rejection is a harsh word.

In Chapter 1 we identified the goal of the recruiter:

'To recruit a person who will quickly start delivering results, who will work happily and harmoniously with colleagues, is keen to learn and develop their role for the benefit of the organisation, is positive and resilient and will be a great ambassador for the organisation.'

They have to choose the best candidate for the role. Not the third best or second best, the best. Remember that the decision matrix recruiters use is largely objective: the candidate does or does not have the required skills and while personality plays an important part, it should by no means be the chief factor in deciding whether a person is able to do a job to the required standard.

If you do not make the next stage of interviews, or you do not get the job, it should be understood that it is not you as a person being rejected, but that someone else more closely matches the requirement.

There is no doubt that it is disappointing when you do not make it through, particularly if there have been several rounds of interviews. While you have taken the advice in the chapter on tackling nerves, about not pinning all your hopes on a single application, you will have visualised success, may have seen yourself in the job and thought about how your life will look and feel if you are successful.

When I worked as a recruitment consultant and whenever I am recruiting, I naturally spend more time telling candidates they have been unsuccessful than the other way around. Nobody likes that part of the job. In the vast majority of cases it is not that the people who didn't make it were not good, far from it, it's that the person who was offered the job had something that just got them over the line first.

This is a chance to see if you could have done anything better by asking for feedback—not all companies will do this, but it's always worth asking. Take the feedback, don't try to change the decision now (trust me, people do), and send an email thanking the company, letting them know you are disappointed, but still interested in working for them should any vacancies arise, if you feel that way.

So, if you are not successful, take any feedback, identify what you can learn from the experience, congratulate yourself on doing a good professional job and move on to the next vacancy.

Success

The ideal situation is you are offered the job. If this happens, there are a few things you need to think about. The first is what you are being offered and what you want, the salary, terms, and start date.

If your instinct is to accept straight away—out of excitement—follow these steps:

- Acknowledge that you are delighted to be offered the job.
- Confirm salary, holidays, any other benefits, and their ideal start date—you should know this from the interview.
- If you are absolutely happy with those terms, and you have been thinking about them throughout the process, by all means accept.
- If you need time to think, tell them that and what time you'll call back—an hour or before 5pm. Do not leave it too long.

Call back and accept, with any tweaks, or decline with a reason.

Declining an offer

During the interview process, it should have been made pretty clear what was on offer should you be successful. Circumstances can change and it is possible you are not offered what you were expecting or your circumstances change meaning you cannot accept the offer—I recommend informing those involved as soon as this looks likely so as not to waste people's time.

Negotiation

In very senior positions, there can be a lot of hardball negotiation involving lawyers, to hammer out a contract and terms and conditions. For most us, we will negotiate our own contracts and, for the most part, the offer will form the terms you will accept.

I urge a degree of caution in negotiating a contract that radically departs from what was clearly on offer from the start—I have known firms withdraw offers when this happens.

There are situations where a candidate makes it very clear from the outset and throughout the process that they are looking for a salary or terms that are outside the parameters set. In this case, some negotiation on the fundamentals is appropriate.

If you want to tweak the terms and conditions, that is fine. For example, you may want to change the start date or ask them to match your current holiday allowance.

Once you are both happy, send an email explicitly accepting the job offer and stating the key terms agreed—in most jurisdictions, you now have a contract.

Counteroffers

In recruitment terms, the counteroffer describes the situation where an existing employer matches or beats the new job offer to retain the member of staff.

For the employee's situation they are bad for the following reason:

Let's say an employee's current salary is 28,000 per annum, the employee is offered 32,000 in a new job and their existing employer counters by offering 33,000 to retain them. This raises a few questions: first, why did this increase not happen before and how long has the employee been undervalued?

Second, it might appear generous, but is in fact retaining the employee on the cheap. Let me explain. To replace a member of staff, there are number of costs, and they are not insignificant.

According to a 2014 UK report by Oxford Economics, the initial cost of replacing a member of staff is £5,433 and that's just the start. The big cost is that of lost output while a replacement employee gets up to speed, said to take around 28 weeks and cost around £25,000.

There is nothing to suggest that it is any different in the Americas, Australasia and Asia. The cost in terms of time, money, and hassle is significant enough to make an apparently generous salary increase incredibly good value, if not cheap.

I would advise companies not to counteroffer as employees who are looking for, interviewing for, and being offered jobs, have their minds on other issues rather than the furtherance of their career with their current employer.

Some candidates will try to get a job offer to stimulate a counteroffer from their employer. This is a very risky tactic. I had a candidate who, it transpired, was playing this game. She received an offer and handed in her notice, which triggered a counteroffer—at this point she had handed in her resignation and not accepted the offer. She then presented the counteroffer to the new company, which rejected it and withdrew their original offer. In the meantime, the existing employer had a change of heart believing it was better just to move on than have an employee who was tempted to look elsewhere. They withdrew the counteroffer and she then had no job—a harsh lesson and a risky tactic. Much easier to ask for a pay rise.

When a recruitment consultant has worked with you and the client to get you over the line, and personnel and managing staff in the hiring company have been working for weeks on the vacancy, it is quite a blow to find the successful candidate was stringing everyone along. It can damage the reputation of the candidate with those parties.

It's why I always ask this question at interviews: *'What would you do if we offered you this position and your current employer offered you more than we are to keep you?'*

A final word on contracts. In most jurisdictions, a contract requires a clear offer and a clear unconditional acceptance to be valid. If it is not clearly accepted, there is no contract and the offer can be withdrawn.

You may hear about conditional offers where the offer is subject to agreement on certain terms or conditional acceptances where the candidate says: *'I accept, subject to agreeing how much commission I'll get.'* Depending on how substantive the condition is, you still don't have a contract until the terms are agreed unequivocally.

Conclusion

In this chapter, you have learnt about:

- Dealing with rejection
- Accepting or declining an offer
- Negotiating and the possible pit falls
- The importance of clearly accepting an offer
- Counteroffers

***

The skills you have learnt can only be used in job interviews. Before I send you on your way, I'll show you why they are life-long skills.

17 What Next?

Remember that there is one thing better than making a living—making a life.

Anonymous

Congratulations. You have made it to the end of the book and, if you follow or have followed the advice, you will either be preparing to start a new job, moving on to the next application or deciding your existing job is not that bad after all.

This brief and final chapter will offer a few words of advice on what to do next with your new knowledge.

Get more out of your job

Remember you have been employed to '*quickly start delivering results, work happily and harmoniously with colleagues, be keen to learn, and develop your role for the benefit of the organisation, be positive and resilient and be a great ambassador for the organisation.*'

But you need to benefit too. It's important to get more out of your work than a pay check at the end of the month:

- So, try to learn new skills
- Learn from the experiences you find yourself in
- Now that you know lots of interview questions, make notes of situations you find yourself in that would answer those questions

- Imagine the perfect CV, what can you do at work to add to it?
- How can you increase your reputation in your industry?

Presentations and persuasion

Use and practise the skills you have learnt in this book in work situations. In a sales environment or presentations requesting money, resources, buy-in to a project or persuading others down a course of action, make sure you have a key message and use the questions you would ask in an interview to cement that message, get more information and overcome objections:

'What was it about the [initial proposal/ discussion document, etc.] that made you want to discuss this further?'

'Is there anything you have heard, or you haven't heard that gives you any doubt about [the success of this project/ our services and products] being right for you?'

Work appraisals

Before a work appraisal it's worth going through the questions in Chapter 10 to focus on strengths, weaknesses, successes, areas for improvement and learning points.

Recruitment

You may be involved in recruiting staff. Chapter 1 sets out a good and solid framework for doing this and the questions in Chapter 9 will help you tease out the required aptitudes and skills.

At the beginning of this book, I set out to help you quickly learn life-changing skills to allow you to be confident in and to master job interviews. We specifically set out to:

- Fully understand the recruitment process from the employer's point of view
- Know how to prepare for an interview
- Identify and develop your selling points into a compelling message

- Understand the different types of interview and how to approach them
- Recognise what any question being asked is aiming to reveal and be able to answer them with confidence
- Have genius questions ready to ask the interviewer that will make you look great
- Be confident about your appearance and body language
- Learn the right amount of communication with the interviewing company to make you look good and not be a nuisance
- Know how to deal with nerves and anxiety
- Learn skills you can use for the rest of your life

I hope we have been successful, and you feel it has been time well spent.

Finally, always be yourself, but be your best, most prepared self.

It only remains for me to wish you the very best for a happy and successful career.

**

I'd love to hear about your interview experiences and questions.

Get in touch: info@job-interview-skills.com

Visit job-interview-skills.com for more interview resources.

Printed in Great Britain
by Amazon